Why
Men
Commit

Why Men Commit

Men explain what it takes to turn a casual relationship into the love of a lifetime

SUSAN CURTIN KELLEY

BOB ADAMS, INC.
· P U B L I S H E R S ·
Holbrook, Massachusetts

Published by Bob Adams, Inc.
260 Center Street, Holbrook, MA 02343

ISBN: 1-55850-159-2

Printed in the United States of America

A   B   C   D   E   F   G   H   I   J

This publication is designed to provide accurate and authoritative information with regard to the subject matter covered. It is sold with the understanding that the publisher is not engaged in rendering legal, accounting, or other professional advice. If legal advice or other expert assistance is required, the services of a qualified professional person should be sought.
— From a *Declaration of Principles* jointly adopted by a Committee of the American Bar Association and a Committee of Publishers and Associations.

The names of the survey respondents quoted in this book are not the names of actual persons.

Cover photo: Adam Smith (Westlight); H. Armstrong Roberts.

To William.

Table of Contents

INTRODUCTION 17

CHAPTER ONE
Men—More than Meets the Eye 21
The communication gap and the new survey that bridges it. What are men looking for? The answers may surprise you.

CHAPTER TWO
When Men Commit 39
He could be everything you want—but if the timing is wrong, back off. First and second marriages: How do men approach them differently?

CHAPTER THREE
Is This Guy for Real? 47
Many women don't give choosing a mate even a fraction of the thought they devote to other, less important issues like buying a car or choosing a piece of furniture. How can you be sure you're dealing with the genuine article?

CHAPTER FOUR

The Committer vs. The Noncommitter 67

A guide to recognizing the man who will commit—and a humorous look at his counterpart who won't.

CHAPTER FIVE

Finding Romance 77

If you wait passively for love to happen, you may bump into your mate in the course of your daily routine . . . or you may find yourself waiting forever.

CHAPTER SIX

The Dos and Don'ts of Seduction 85

Is that elusive quality we call "the right chemistry" truly spontaneous . . . or can you help it to develop?

CHAPTER SEVEN

The Commitment 99

You will win your chosen man by fulfilling a need or needs that have not been met in his former intimate relationships. Here's the step-by-step formula that will show you how.

CHAPTER EIGHT

Getting Smart With Strategic Planning 111

Strategic planning is knowing where you want to be within a certain time frame—and understanding what you have to do to get there. Learn how this concept applies to romance just as well as it does to one's work life.

CHAPTER NINE

    Making It Happen **119**

    Bringing the relationship to where you want it to be . . . by setting the date for your wedding.

CHAPTER TEN

    Trial Commitment **127**

    How to handle a negative response? Work within your own schedule and set definite target dates for a final decision on commitment.

CHAPTER ELEVEN

    In Their Own Words **133**

    Men describe commitments that clicked.

APPENDIX A

    Questions You Should Ask a Man Who Hasn't Yet Committed **143**

APPENDIX B

    Highlights from the Survey **159**

APPENDIX C

    Questionnaire for Those Approaching Marriage **167**

APPENDIX D

    Bibliography/Recommended Reading **173**

INDEX **179**

Acknowledgments

I'd like to thank my editor, Brandon Toropov, for first believing in this project. Others who helped this book along at Bob Adams, Inc., include Chris Ciaschini, Kate Layzer, Lisa Fisher, and Matt Keenan.

To the men I interviewed, who were wonderfully candid and eager to share their views and experiences, I wish to extend my sincere gratitude.

Special thanks go to my army of friends and relatives who helped with the nationwide commitment survey canvassing.

I especially wish to thank my husband William, whose love, support, and good humor made this book possible. To him, I am gratefully and eternally committed.

*"We must plan . . . or we
must perish."*
— Howard Laski (1893–1950)

Introduction

This book is for every woman who wants to get married. *Why Men Commit* discloses the *real* reasons men commit to relationships and shows you how to guide your man toward your ultimate goal of marriage.

What will make the man in your life want to commit to you instead of to the last woman he was involved with . . . or, perhaps, the next? What will inspire him to change or deepen a relationship that he happily maintains at status quo? Is there something you can do to speed up the process to reach your goal of marriage? Yes!

Why Men Commit delves into the minds of men and reveals startling results from a new national survey about why men choose a particular mate. You will find out what characteristics and qualities all men seek from their partner. Based on returns from this recent questionnaire, you will learn how men change their perspective on sex, finances, and appearance between their first marriage and their second.

● ● ●

A close correlation exists between managing professional and personal relationships. In performing your job as well as in the day-to-day running of your life, you have to learn what people want and need before you can meet their needs. This concept easily transfers to the personal relationships between men and women. By approaching your relationship with logic and common sense as well as emotion, you can put yourself more in control of the course your love life takes.

Why Men Commit allows you to see the world through men's eyes. When you understand the reasons why men commit, you will be capable of fitting yourself within those guidelines.

The potential for enjoying a successful relationship already exists within you.

If your way isn't working for you, if you have not been successful in getting your man to commit, then you will benefit from reading this book. First, you may have to unlearn some habits that have been obstacles to reaching your goal of marriage. By understanding what men are really looking for in their mate, you will know how to meet those needs. You may need to learn how to recognize the right person when you find him or how to listen more and talk less or how to ask the right questions about values and past relationships.

Why Men Commit will show you how to take a proven, intellectual approach, develop a strategy, and apply it to your relationship with the man of your choice.

This guide presents a sophisticated approach for a woman who's in charge of her life and going after what she wants—a commitment from her man.

CHAPTER ONE

Men: More than Meets the Eye

*"I was looking for a best
friend."*

— Doug

"It was time to settle down." What does a man mean when he says this? Does a woman have any influence over the development of this attitude in a man? If she has done her homework; if she is in a good relationship; if the chemistry is there . . . is there a way to make a man feel this way? Just as important, what must she *avoid* doing?

●   ●   ●

In interviewing the men whose stories are recounted here, I learned more about the way the male mind works than I ever expected to. As it turned out, some of my preconceptions about the way men deal with deciding to commit were completely at odds with reality. You may find yourself having an equally eye-opening experience as you read this book.

For most women, the study I conducted will be fascinating reading. For a great many the results will be more than an interesting diversion; this book's emphasis on the three primary reasons men commit, and how to plan accordingly, can save women untold frustration and emotional distress. Read on—they're probably not the reasons you think they are!

For my part, I should say that I was as surprised as anyone at the responses I received. I honestly do not know exactly what motivated my subjects to discuss their lives with me on such an intimate level. The point is, they did—and the book you are holding in your hands should be, I believe, required reading for every woman who plans to marry.

● ● ●

Once you understand why men commit and what your special man's needs are, you can follow a simple, proven strategy that will make your man *want* to commit to you. That is the key, of course; getting the man himself to feel inspired to commit to the relationship. There is a closer correlation than most of us admit between managing professional relationships and personal ones. In the day-to-day job that is life, you have to learn what people want and need before you can meet their needs or expect them to meet yours. This concept, which is essential to conducting a board meeting, managing the family finances effectively, or getting a teenager to clean up her room, also has everything in the world to do with the personal relationships of men and women.

By approaching your relationship with the same logic and clearheadedness you use in other areas of your life, you can complement the emotional components of your relationship (not eradicate them!)—and put yourself more in control of the course of your love life.

Using logic and common sense, though, is easier said than done. No one *tries* to exclude these things from a relationship with a man: We simply find ourselves confused because we do not understand what the other side is thinking. That's where this book comes in. *Why Men Commit* will allow you to see the world through men's eyes. Once you understand the reasons men commit, reasons they don't usually talk about with their prospective mates, you will be in a better position to plan your next step.

THE COMMUNICATION GAP

The interviews I conducted showed an astonishing gap in communication between the sexes. Expectations that women think men have for them often do not exist.

Many women are striving to fulfill an ideal that is their own perception, not a man's, of what the opposite sex wants and needs. Why do so many women undergo breast augmentation surgery, for instance? Because they assume men will find them more attractive. Yet only one man of the hundreds upon hundreds interviewed for this book said that he committed to a woman because of her ample breast size!

Perhaps you are skeptical; perhaps you feel that I was, for whatever reason, misled by my interviewees, or that men are not the best judges of what will attract their own kind. I reacted in much the same way until I began to discuss these issues in depth with my subjects. Consider these comments from Doug, a 42-year-old photographer.

Q. Can you describe the importance of a woman's body as a part of your decision to commit?

A. Well, it certainly didn't top my list. I mean, breasts are something you look at on the beach. But you don't marry a woman because she has large breasts, though a lot of women seem to think that's the big deal for a man. I was looking for a best friend.

Most men agree that although a pleasing physical appearance may have been a significant factor in the initial attraction and in developing a relationship, it was *not* their reason for committing. Furthermore, many men have a distinct preference for small-breasted women. There are as many preferences as there are men.

In looking anew at this issue—and at countless others—I couldn't help thinking that if this communication gap could be closed—if women only knew what really made men commit—they could follow a more realistic plan. The women would feel more confident and have a better opportunity to create satisfying partnerships.

Let's acknowledge a difficult truth. For many women, romance or the prospect of it brings a giddy, emotional gush of irrationality that leads nowhere. I have seen far too many intelligent members of my sex lose their clearheaded, analytical approach to life when a man enters the picture. As a result, we get into relationships only to get disappointed and hurt later. If men, as a group, have certain (often surprising!) ways of making decisions when it comes to marrying—and they do—we should know about those tendencies before we act.

And what better way to find the real answers than to go directly to the source and ask married men why they committed?

● ● ●

The men you will meet in these pages have been enthusiastic and candid in their responses to my questions. For many men, it was their first opportunity to discuss the issue of commitment, and they took full advantage of it. One 52-year-old biologist actually said to me after filling out my questionnaire, "I wish I'd met you on different terms. I never realized I hated my wife until I filled this out." For the most part, however, the responses were positive.

The age range of the men sharing their stories was twenty-three to eighty-two years. Their educational level ran from high-school dropouts to graduates of universities, medical schools, and business schools. The subjects include physicians, dentists, CEO's, farmers, veterinarians, mailmen, executives, engineers, musicians, entertainers, professional baseball players, artists, writers, and retirees.

The survey results break through the male mystique and allow us to see men as they really are—and they are not the incomprehensible, mercurial creatures some women believe them to be.

WHAT ARE MEN LOOKING FOR?

The top three reasons given by the men I spoke to for committing to marriage finished so closely that they should be considered as a group. Companionship, love, and sexual fulfillment head the list.

In a way, the close finish is telling. What men are saying, I believe is this: They are looking for *a best friend who is also a loyal, trusting partner with whom they can have great sex.*

That's the ideal, and it is notable primarily for what it does not include. Consider the following stereotypical summaries of what some women *think* men are looking for in a wife, and note how little they have in common with the top three reasons men actually give.

WHAT DIDN'T MAKE THE LIST OF THINGS THAT MAKE MEN COMMIT?

- Physical beauty.

- Ideal weight.

- Willingness to shoulder most child care duties.

- Willingness to postpone or abandon career goals.

- Common socioeconomic or religious background.

- Willingness or ability to perform housework or cook.*

The good news is that the majority of the married men surveyed said they would marry the same woman again. Sam, a 49-year-old actor, grinned when asked

---

* It should be noted that, within contemporary marriages, a number of studies have shown that women continue to do most of a family's housework, even in two-income households. Our purpose here, however, is to identify those factors important *to men* in considering whether or not to marry; my feeling after reviewing the survey is that, these days, a woman's willingness or ability to perform domestic chores simply is not on the wish list of most modern men. Whether or not that translates to an enthusiastic participation in housekeeping tasks during the marriage itself is, of course, another matter.

this question and said, "Remarry the same woman? I did!" His was not the only case of a marriage that came back to life after legal separation or divorce.

Following are some of the most common answers men give when asked, "Why did you commit?"

> *"She's my best friend."* (This was the single most common response!)
>
> *"She was the right person at the right time."*
>
> *"She makes me feel good."*
>
> *"I felt I wanted to settle down."*
>
> *"We wanted to start a family."*
>
> *"We enjoy overall compatibility."*
>
> *"She asked me."*
>
> *"She was too much of a gem for me to risk losing."*

Virtually none of the respondents committed for financial reasons, and in no case was this even a factor in a first marriage.

COMPANIONSHIP

Men need to be in the company of women, and, in particular, in the company of a female love companion. This is a simple fact that too many women ignore; they consider that men are in the driver's seat, or that they, women, are "sellers" in a "buyer's market." Such formulations gloss over the fact that men have emotional and social needs, too. Those needs are powerful motivators in the decision to commit.

As Martin, a 45-year-old florist marrying for the second time, put it,

> *"I needed someone to be with. I had to have a sense that there was a mutual respect, that we could share our feelings together and be secure in both our own identities and our identity as a couple. I would marry Sharon again—primarily because she provided that for me."*

Or listen to James, a 50-year-old performer married for sixteen years:

> *"It was the differences between us that were key as far as I was concerned. She complemented me so well. Together, we're kinder, better tempered, and probably more intelligent people."*

LOVE

Webster's gives not one but three relevant definitions for the word "love": "intense affection," "a feeling of attraction arising from desire," and "enthusiasm or fondness." Whatever love is, it matters a great deal more to men than women imagine. Interview after interview unearthed deep emotional attachments and affection as a primary factor in a man's decision to commit.

It may not come as a surprise that most men citing love as their primary motivation in committing did not wax eloquent on exactly what they meant by that statement. But there were a number of revealing comments men made that can shed some light on the issue:

> *"Sure, I went out with other women—but I only found out what the story was when I met Dianne. The rest—forget 'em. She's my first and last love. The real thing. The genuine article."* (Bill, a 31-year-old nurse.)

> *"Living in separate cities nearly drove me nuts. That's what really brought it home for me. I wasn't sure if it really felt like the right one until we had to be apart for a while—then I knew. Whatever love was supposed to be, this had to be it. Laurie was the right one. I felt I missed her so much that if we didn't get married I wouldn't be able to stand it."* (Andrew, a 24-year-old computer programmer.)

> *"She was everything I needed. I don't know if I can put it any more clearly than that. She filled all the holes."* (Ryan, a 64-year-old aerospace engineer.)

SEXUAL FULFILLMENT
The overwhelming majority of men I spoke to rated sexual fulfillment as a very important factor in com-

mitting to marriage. A satisfying sexual relationship makes a man feel important and strengthens his self-confidence. A good many men committed primarily because a regular sex partner was important.

When asked what makes a woman a good lover, Paul, a 30-year-old consultant, emphasized intimacy and communication over any *Playboy*-inspired conceptions of sexuality:

> *"(I looked for) sensitivity; knowing where to touch and how to touch."*

Most men I interviewed said that the best lover is a woman who responds to and enjoys sex herself. If that doesn't count as a pleasant surprise, nothing does. A servile or performance-oriented mentality, then, is out, and no trapezes or bizarre positions are required. The majority of men, because they themselves get something back from your pleasure, simply want to relax and enjoy the mutual pleasure of love-making.

And what makes a woman *not* a good lover?

> *"That's easy,"* said Jack, a 35-year-old artist. *"A woman who's inhibited; who doesn't want to relax and go with the flow . . . . Sex is important to me and it has to be very, very good sex, otherwise there's no use in establishing a long-term relationship."*

Of course, there were other factors that ranked high in the survey besides the Big Three of companionship, love, and sexual fulfillment. Here is a brief overview.

SENSE OF HUMOR

Most men agreed that a sense of humor is crucial to any relationship. Over 70 percent rated it as very important in their overall commitment decision. Several men said that a sense of humor was even more important than sex. This should not be taken to mean that the average man is looking to marry a stand-up comic, a woman who plays practical jokes or throws a pie in his face when he walks through the door at the end of the day. Men, more than women, are guarded all day long. They are looking for a companion with whom they can let their guard down. They want to be on the same wavelength with someone, and if both partners laugh at the same things, that's a good indication that that goal has been achieved.

When men place emphasis on a woman's sense of humor, they are really highlighting the importance of the communication process. Humor is a vital part of any peer-oriented relationship; this is one of the reasons relationships in which the partners must bridge a large age gap can be problematic.

When the woman or the man is considerably younger, they often can't relate to the same things— and, not insignificantly, don't get the same jokes.

We all want to be around people who help us forget the trials, tribulations, stresses, and strains of everyday life. As Mark, a 23-year-old law student, put it,

"Bad things happen. You have to be able to laugh."

Fred, a 33-year-old restaurant owner said,

"Everything can get boring . . . (except) a sense of humor."

According to Joe, a 32-year-old consultant,

"A sense of humor is important to people like me. I'm outgoing, I like people, I like to laugh and to have a good time. I like to lighten up life. I enjoy people who have a sense of humor and I don't like to be around people who don't have a sense of humor, people who take themselves or the whole world too seriously. I like wit; it's fun. Generally, people with a sense of humor are fairly bright. A witty person can see the lighter side of life."

EMOTIONAL STABILITY

It's not so much that a man consciously looks for emotional stability in the same way he would look for other characteristics in a woman; he assumes that that stability is there. And he will often terminate the relationship if he finds evidence that it is not.

For a man, emotional stability is something you assume is there, something to be taken for granted. If a woman is attractive and bright and has a sense of humor, a man will usually not question her emotional makeup. Emotional problems that are discovered comparatively late in the game can make the difference between a man's committing or his abandoning the relationship.

An emotionally stable person is basically even-tempered and in control; he or she does not experience a lot of ups and downs in everyday life. A person who is emotionally unstable has a lot of peaks and valleys and is very difficult to live with, and most men know this.

Ed, aged 27, said,

"The best example of emotional instability I can give you is my wife's PMS I feel like I'm dealing with a dual personality. Had I witnessed this prior to my marriage, I honestly think I would have had second thoughts."

No man will look forward to living in dread anticipation of mood swings and temper outbursts; that's why it's so important to understand yourself, to be in control of your life. Make an effort to find healthy ways to vent your anxiety, be it through exercise or psychotherapy. Remember, you want him to stay committed, and virtually all men consider emotional fits frightening and unacceptable behavior.

APPEARANCE

Physical attraction is an important part of any marriage, but most men aren't looking for beauty queens. A pleasing overall appearance, based on the individual's own esthetic, is what men find important in the commitment process.

In rating the importance of individual features, the eyes have it. Over 60 percent of men rated eyes as a woman's most important feature.

> *"I remember reading once that the eyes are the mirror of the soul,"* said Leo, a portrait painter, *"and I think that's particularly true of women."*

Tastes vary, of course. Benjamin, a 50-year-old fashion photographer, said, "Cheek bones are the most important feature, along with eyes and, of course, mouth." He'd been married three times and was back looking. "I'm a sucker for cheek bones. I can't seem to get by that."

In general, most men are enticed by a look that complements, rather than distorts, one's natural features. As Drake, an editor, put it,

> *"A woman should be what she is; too many of them plaster themselves with makeup, which I find very unattractive. A very subtle makeup job that accentuates a few key features is much more attractive to me than someone trying to pretend she's something she isn't."*

BACK TO THE BIG THREE

While considerations such as a sense of humor, emotional stability, and appearance may be important secondary considerations for many men, the most important primary principles remain those of companionship, love, and sexual fulfillment. To be perceived as an exceptional partner/provider in these areas requires that a woman be secure in her sense of self and confident about the kind of man she will be happy living with. They cannot be faked for any period of time, though many people do endure unhappy marriages that do not feature these elements. You should not be one of them.

Brad, a 40-year-old computer programmer, does a great job of summing up the commonalities for committing:

> *"I wanted a best friend, a great lover, and a trusting companion. I found this in my spouse, and I think of her every day."*

It is this kind of match we will be focusing on in this book.

STRATEGIES FOR COMMITMENT

You can help the man of your choice reach the decision that you are the life partner he has been looking for. Failing that, you can determine once and for all that the man in question is not the kind to commit at all—and move on all the sooner to someone who is right for you and *will* commit.

And what if you don't have a special man in your life right now? *Why Men Commit* will teach you to implement methods used in other areas of your everyday routine, so you can learn how to search out likely candidates, select the best bachelors, narrow your decision down to one man, and, finally, get that man to commit. You will also learn how to identify and avoid dead-end relationships that virtually *never* end in successful commitment.

It is a myth that none of the "good men out there" want to commit to marriage. However, men sometimes need something or someone to provide the impetus that will make taking that "big step" possible for them. In this book, you will learn how to provide that impetus.

CHAPTER TWO

When Men Commit

> *"I was looking for a
> co-pilot, not a passenger,
> the second time."*
>
> — Grady

He could be everything you want, a great catch and a wonderful match, but . . . he's recently divorced or separated and needs to go through the healing process. Or he may be completely focused on his career or just too young to make a lifelong commitment. It may be possible to wait until he's ready, but in the long run it might be better for you to get out now and find another man whose timing is better.

While waiting at the airport, I recently made the acquaintance of a young man of 28. I was meeting my husband; this fellow was anxiously anticipating the arrival of his girlfriend. The flight was delayed, and we started to talk. He told me he loved his girlfriend, but she was 32 and pressuring him to get married. She wanted to start a family right away.

> *"Her clock is running,"* he explained. *"But I'm just too young. I'm having a great time and I'm not even sure I want kids, but I don't think I do."*

This is a classic example of two people who love each other but are not at the same place at the same time. She's ready; he's definitely not. He may not be for another ten years. Marriage would be a big mistake for both of them.

Pressures are very different for men and women. Men can start families in their forties, fifties, and beyond. Women are biologically much more limited, and—news flash!—this puts a huge demographic squeeze on a lot of females.

Women in a promising situation often don't want to hear it, but it is best for everyone if men commit only when they feel they are ready. Often, however, by knowing how men think and what they are facing you can make it easier for your potential mate to feel he is ready. We'll be examining techniques that will help you do just this throughout the book.

But first, a little background. There are definite times in a man's life when he's more susceptible to marriage. But how can a woman *know* when the time is right? Through open communication, you can judge for yourself. If he's struggling with career goals, it's probably not a good time for him. If he's still working out financial and emotional problems over alimony and child support, perhaps he hasn't separated emotionally from his former wife. If you glean through discussions that he's followed negative patterns in previous relationships, if he's angry, hate-filled, or depressed or doesn't seem to be making headway with working through his feelings, he may need professional counseling to break those patterns. And those patterns *must* be broken before he can move on to a new and healthy relationship.

If you believe he needs professional counseling but he vehemently resists the idea, you may want to move on to another man. On the other hand, if he is willing to go to see a counselor, you will have to decide whether you want to get involved in the rehabilitation process—and that includes going to the therapy sessions with him, if he and the counselor request it.

Keep in mind that there are plenty of emotionally healthy, available men around who are ready to commit. It's dangerous to push a man into a commitment if he is not ready. It can—and often does—backfire and destroy the relationship forever.

Take the case of Brian, one of the men I interviewed for this book. Brian and Linda had been living together since college. Years passed, and Linda was worried that her biological clock was running out of time. She wanted to get married and start a family, but Brian kept backing off. He was already feeling pressured from starting a new business; that was his priority for the moment.

Linda thought she could force the issue by becoming pregnant. But, to her amazement, when she told Brian she was pregnant, he responded defensively. He asked (as many frightened men in that situation ask), "How do I know it's my child?"

Most women would feel betrayed when asked that question, and Linda, hurt and angry, was no exception. Unfortunately, men do not see the issue in quite this light. If the man's initial problem is one of feeling pressured, compounding that pressure with the prospect of instant—and unsought—fatherhood generally only makes matters worse. The man will search for a reason not to have to assume the responsibility for which he feels ill prepared.

As it turned out, Linda was not pregnant—but the relationship was over. Had Linda been patient, she would probably have gotten Brian to commit once his business was established.

Most men won't jump into a commitment . . . but they can be gently prodded toward it if the time is right. And *no* man wants marriage shoved at him when he is clearly not ready. A man must have prior relationships worked through, and he must not be dealing with other major changes in his life that drain his energy. After all, the goal is for both of you to *stay* happily committed.

Interestingly, the vast majority of the survey respondents who answered that they would *not* marry the same woman again had married for one or more of the following forced reasons: pregnancy, ultimatums from the woman, or family pressures.

FIRST MARRIAGES

Many couples marry for the first time because infatuation and passion overwhelm them. Sometimes partners marry in order to fulfill other people's expectations or because society has told them it's the right thing to do. Background and family pressures can play a large part in the decision-making process, especially when they are young and trying to please those close to them. Even here, however, successful marriages are notable for the degree of common assent and, specifically, by the man's sense at the time that he is ready to take the step of marriage.

Men know that every relationship comes to a point where you have to make a decision. As Dan, a 31-year-old systems engineer, explained, "(Marriage) was the next logical step." Peter, a 23-year-old shipping clerk, married because "I felt it was time after three years of dating."

Timing may play a role. James, a 31-year-old carpenter, said, "I wanted to settle down and start a family." Often, a man will realize that if he doesn't marry his significant other, somebody else may. "I didn't want to lose her," said Frank, a 40-year-old accountant.

The first time around, a man tends to marry a woman who fits into his preconceived notion of what a wife should be. The mold he expects her to fit is one that's been in existence almost since the day he discovered the difference between men and women.

Of course, for members of both sexes, unrealistic expectations often accompany the first commitment. You're in love, everything is bliss; you anticipate a conflict-free marriage and don't foresee making accommodations. How could you ever imagine that your love's endearing habits could turn into petty annoyances? It's possible that you may even neglect to discuss major issues like career goals or whether you want children. There's an innocence as we enter a first marriage, and we assume that we marry for all the right motives. We assume it is forever. Often, however, it is not.

SECOND MARRIAGES

Second marriages tend to be more calculated. After you've been through one divorce, there is no innocence. Considerations that were not present the first time factor into the decision-making process. A man may bring to a second marriage all the pain and the emotional baggage from the first. There may be no escaping such complications.

For better or for worse, he's looking for different things. He may still be attracted to tall redheads, but if he married one and was burned by that first love, he may never consider a tall redhead again, even though she may be absolutely suited for him.

My research shows that, in second marriages, men tended to feel more stable and mature than the first time around. They are more clear about what they want or don't want. Jim, an engineer from Michigan, said, "In my second marriage, I was looking for someone who wanted a family and wanted to be a wife." You may not agree with Jim (most of the men I interviewed didn't), but the fact is, he knew exactly what he was looking for. If you know what a man wants, you can decide whether your needs are compatible with his.

New criteria may be introduced, all based on the man's past experience. Furthermore, although love and companionship, the main incentives for committing in second marriages, parallel those of the first, two important new stipulations are introduced the second time.

The most significant of these is money. Most men maintain that their wives' financial status was not a consideration in the first marriage. In the second marriage, however, that changes. Men are generally not looking for financial dependents at this stage of their lives.

"I was looking for a co-pilot, not a passenger, the second time," said Grady, a 44-year-old salesman. "I wanted a more equally balanced situation than the first time. I got tired of paying the mortgage and all the bills myself." In a second marriage, men are more likely to discuss ahead of time the issue of who pays for what.

The second new condition looked for in a second wife was that she have an identity as a working person. Many men whose first wives had not worked outside the home said that they wanted their second wife to do so. They appreciated the stimulation and energy of the working wife after, to use some typical language from the interviews, the "boredom" and "submission" of the first.

Often, however, a man may simply desire the opposite of what he experienced the first time. If he had a stay-at-home wife, he might be looking for a career woman, and vice versa. Jake, 44, said his reasons for committing the second time were different. "My first wife was a stiff; my second wife is bright, a great lover, and my favorite golf partner."

The guiding principle for second-time-around men, though, is that they have a clear idea of what they want and are unwilling to repeat past errors. Stanley, an advertising executive, said that he proposed to his second wife four months after he met her because he was in love. "But this time I did what I wanted, not what was expected of me." Barry, a 32-year-old teacher, said, "I was ready to commit and was realistic this time."

For the most part, men are more in charge of their lives and know themselves better when the opportunity presents itself for a second marriage. They feel less pressured by outside forces. They are looking for a woman to enhance life and make it more pleasant. They are less likely to be swayed by externals or outside pressure.

CHAPTER THREE

Is This Guy for Real?

> *"I am the leader of the
> boys."*
>
> — Michael

When a woman is ready for marriage, she doesn't want to invest a lot of her time and an essential element of herself in a dead-end relationship. But how do you know if the man in question will commit?

There is no definite way of knowing, but if you allow the relationship to unfold in a natural way and approach it with the same common sense that you use in other areas of your life, you will have a better feeling for whether or not the man is on the level. *If he is serious, he'll be willing to take it slow.*

We're talking here about one of the most important decisions you're ever going to make: choosing a partner with whom you will want to spend the rest of your life. And yet many women don't give the matter even a fraction of the thought they devote to other, less important issues. Before you buy a TV, a car, or a house, or find day care for your two-year old, you research the possibilities thoroughly and systematically. You certainly *don't* accept at face value every claim the salesperson makes without checking the track record.

You examine the practicality and the fit. You want to be certain that what you're going to end up with will suit your needs. In romance, too, you have to act intelligently. You have to stay in control. And you have to protect yourself.

"THE ONE"

You meet a man and feel instant attraction. You think he could be *the one*. You begin to date. It's all going very well; he says all the right words: He's never met anyone like you, he loves you, he wants to spend his life with you. He may allude to future events in an intimate, enticing way. Perhaps you're at a party with some friends, there is a humorous incident, and he leans over to you and says softly, "We'll be laughing at this in years to come."

It sounds wonderful—but is it live, or is it Memorex?

He's courting you. In our society this activity is, in large measure, a prelude to having sex. Bear that in mind. His flattery and his implications do not necessarily mean he's interested in a longtime commitment.

You will need to train yourself to look at your

man objectively and intelligently in an effort to ascertain whether or not he is for real. This can be tricky— especially when he comes on strong and seems to be speaking from the heart. Men often consider it their part of the bargain to lay the lines on thick and fast; they often see nothing wrong with being a bit insincere in the process. Women, however, usually don't say things to men about emerging relationships unless they're meant. Therefore, many women accept as truth things we could call, depending on our outlook, either lies or unfortunate, heat-of-the-moment insincerities. We must remember that the men telling them may consider themselves to be simply acting out "the talking part" of the game.

● ● ●

According to large statistical samplings of men, there are things a woman can do and say at certain stages of a relationship that will virtually always turn a man off. One of those things is "pushing too hard, too soon." Men, of course, do quite a bit of energetic negotiating themselves early in relationships, but that seems not to enter into the thinking. They can push; we can't. It's not equal; it's not fair; it is, however, what you have to know to play the game successfully without being hurt.

Samantha, a 40-year-old advertising executive, met Dick, a business tycoon, while attending a wedding reception. He pursued her relentlessly for the next week until she agreed to have dinner with him.

Even before that first dinner, he was dropping hints. He had, he mentioned, paid her the ultimate tribute of programming her telephone number into his car phone.

"Where," he asked her on the first date, "have you been all my life?" Later, he called her three times a day, heaping praise on every aspect of her personality, appearance, and past history. She felt, she admitted, like a teenager again. The second date, he kept up the assault: "I want to spend the rest of my life with you." It was powerful stuff. They slept together the third week.

Samantha couldn't believe it was all happening so fast. Dick insisted on getting her two children together with his son. Samantha agreed, despite a nagging feeling that such a step was premature. After two months, though, things seemed to be going remarkably well. Dick was saying subtle things like, "It's wonderful to be together with the kids like this; it's just like we're a real family."

After two months of such intimate sharing, with green lights seemingly flashing at every corner, Samantha made a passing reference to the possibility of getting married—and the relationship was over as suddenly as it began.

Dick stopped calling; when Samantha called him, she found he wasn't so sure about that ski trip they'd planned. He needed some time to himself. He had to sort things out. He was, he said, scared.

"Of what?" asked Samantha.

"Of getting close," he answered.

And he was. As hurt and as angry as Samantha

felt—as any woman in such a situation would feel—the plain fact is, men often don't understand the seriousness with which their signals are taken. We must sometimes do the thinking for them, and must keep things progressing at a slower, steadier pace than they might initially like.

Samantha would probably have been better off had she controlled the relationship instead of allowing it to control her. Then she would have gotten to know Dick a little better before making the emotional investment she did. As it happened, she allowed herself to become swept up in a blinding romance in which the man controlled virtually every aspect of timing and progression. Because of the promises, spoken and unspoken, that Dick made, Samantha entered into a sexual relationship when she knew she was not emotionally ready for it. For her, however, the physical involvement constituted commitment, and she naturally assumed that Dick was equally committed.

After they broke up, Samantha learned from a third party that she had been a pretty typical relationship for Dick. He didn't have many close or long-term friends; instead, he was surrounded by short-term associates. With Samantha, he saw what he wanted and went after it just as he would in a business setting: with great passion. When she responded, he felt trapped and didn't want her any more. The chase was over. There was no challenge anymore.

Dick's case is a good one to examine closely. It is easiest, of course, to look back on the progression of that relationship and declare that Dick had been lying from the first day on. But had he?

Most likely, Dick had legitimate feelings for Samantha when the romance began; he was simply incapable of acting on those feelings in a mature manner. Whether he admitted it to himself or not, he was happiest in the role of the hunter. For Dick, truth was (and, probably still is) a moment-to-moment affair. Given more time, Samantha might have learned that before she got hurt.

In romance, as in other areas of life, it is a good idea to listen to your instincts. Let time and a slowly developing relationship dictate whether what a man says to you is true or a line. If he means what he says, what's the rush? He'll hang in there if he really does love you. Why not prolong that most wonderful and exciting stage of a relationship—the passion- filled courtship?

LEARNING TO LISTEN

Listen more; talk less. Men need this change of approach. It makes the early stages of the relationship easier for them. (How many men have you heard complaining that women talk too *little*?) More important, listening will give you the opportunity to find out exactly who you're dealing with.

Stop trying to prove your worth and concentrate more on whether or not the man is what you want and need. Learn to ask questions that will allow you to get to know the real man and his values. Go beyond "What do you do?"—find out about his attitude toward life, his dealings with other people. Does he, for instance, have friendships that he's maintained for longer than six months? If not, look long and hard before you leap!

Try to meet someone who has had a long-term relationship with this person (not necessarily a romantic relationship). Subtly ask about his past association. Pay attention to the overall patterns of your man's past.

Through careful listening, you will learn to recognize the real man when you find him. You will know when not to invest your effort and energy.

● ● ●

"He says he'll never leave his wife, but I know he will if I wait long enough."

Joan, a 45-year-old TV producer, has been in a frustrating and unhappy relationship with Tom for over five years. Tom is the married father of five; he is politically involved, active in the community, and earns a good income as an advertising executive. He is, Joan says, a great lover. She does not want to end the relationship.

Tom has not lied to Joan. He has honestly stated that he will never leave his wife. But this isn't what Joan wants to hear. So she waits—unhappily—on the slender hope that he does not mean what he says.

● ● ●

Alan and Maureen have been living together for three years; they met just one month after Maureen's first marriage ended in a messy divorce. Maureen had heard stories of Alan's womanizing before they moved in together, and she was a little uneasy about committing to him so quickly after the divorce. But she felt she needed the tenderness and caring he provided, qualities that had been sorely lacking in her marriage. At a vulnerable point in her life, she moved in with him and hoped for the best.

She now has strong suspicions that he has been seeing other women; they have had several fights about it. She wants to get married—he always says "next year" will be the best time. Two years have passed.

● ● ●

If you really listen when a man talks, you will know, one way or another, whether he is worth pursuing. You will know if he is on the level, whether you can trust what he says. Remember that you are trying to determine three things:

- ● Is this man likely to commit?

- ● If so, what set of needs is he trying to satisfy?

- ● Will it be to our mutual advantage for him to conclude that I can fulfill those needs?

Of course, your needs are crucial, as well—but our purpose here is to get inside your man's head, to see what yardsticks he will be using in contemplating potential partners. Once you get a "yes" answer to that third question (and it may well take time), you will know that you are dealing with "the real thing"—and you can act accordingly.

The real problems arise when women either know or have strong suspicions that they are being lied to—or will be lied to—yet go on as though nothing were wrong. Too often, women lock themselves into unsatisfying or unhealthy relationships because they listen only for key phrases. So he says he loves you; so what? He could say he owns the Brooklyn Bridge; would you buy it? What do his *actions* say about him?

Just as dangerous is the fatal error of assuming that the man does not mean what he says when he tells you he cannot or will not commit to you. Ah, but what if . . . ? Perhaps you can rescue him/become the most important thing in his life/change his outlook, but you probably can't. If he is honest enough with you to give you the real story, don't hang on. Keep in mind exactly what kind of man we are talking about here. This is not the one who honestly wants to advance professionally so he can start a family, the one who tells you, "I can't get married unless I get a better job." We are talking here about the gentleman who looks you straight in the eye and says, "Before we go any further, I want you to know what you're getting into here; I am not getting married again. Period." If you don't want to conduct the relationship under those terms—don't!

There are a lot of great guys out there who want to commit to the right woman. There's a man for you, too. If you listen, you'll know when you find him. Don't be a victim. Train yourself to spot the noncommitters early on. Stay in control of your life.

LEARNING TO SPOT THE DANGER SIGNALS

The presence of any one of these signals after half a year together is not necessarily an indicator of trouble—but if five to seven apply to your relationship, you should think twice before continuing with the man. Six months represents a pretty good base-line measure of whether the relationship is going in the direction you want. If, after that time, you can't seem to make any emotional progress, you're probably not going to. Watch the signs.

- He still refers to everything as "mine" (even such communal items as toilet paper); he discusses what *he* will be doing in the future, rather than using the plural *"we."*

- He frequently appears interested in other women when you're together.

- He asks you to make a significant change in your appearance by altering your hair color, nose, breast size, etc.

- He still lives with his parents in their home.

- You haven't met any of his friends or family members.

- You wonder if you'll be doing something together on the weekend, but wait for him to bring it up.

- (If he is divorced:) He talks frequently of his ex-wife and leaves open the possibility of their getting back together.

- (If he is separated:) He has been separated from his wife for a number of years but has made no effort to initiate divorce proceedings.

- He always drives.

- He always picks the movie or other entertainment.

- He always orders the entree.

- He is always on top.

MEN WHO WON'T COMMIT

What to do if you know your man is unlikely to commit? Be smart and do the positive thing: move on. Don't waste time on him.

How can you tell, though, whether you're facing nothing more than a healthy "delaying" response in a man who really does want to go with a relationship? It is true that many worthwhile men possess very active "delay hormones." Still, you *can* separate these men from the absolute noncommitters.

Following are some common profiles of men who will not commit. Some will be familiar; other types are so subtle you may not have considered them before. Of course, noncommitters come in all shapes and sizes and display a multitude of behaviors, but the following summaries will give you a good basic idea of the kinds of men to watch out for.

The Prince of Pain

He's recently separated and in the throes of an ugly divorce. He sees himself as being persecuted; he can talk of little else. He may need a therapist or a nurse, but a new wife will not solve his problems. Whether he knows it or not, he's not ready to commit.

The Liar

He claims he's not married and never has been, but there's a tan line on the ring finger of his left hand. He's often late for dates. Sometimes he cancels them altogether at the last minute. You spend hurricanes and holidays alone. He's already committed.

The Cheater

He's busy every Friday and Saturday night. He can only see you on Thursdays and Sundays. He won't admit that he's seeing anyone else, but he won't keep a weekend open for you, either. Pressed, he will ask *which* weekend night you want. He may not be married, but he's emotionally incapable of committing.

The "Great Catch"

He's successful (a lawyer or dentist, say) and seems perfect. He's over 45, but has never been married or been in a serious relationship. (He claims not to have met the "right type" yet.) He lives alone (well, with a cat). He has complete sets of linens, glassware, flatware, and furnishings. He is meticulous and becomes upset if anything is disturbed. This fellow is not going to be nesting with you or anyone else; he is set for life, a confirmed bachelor. There is no room for another person in his well-ordered universe.

The Hider

He's afraid to get involved, so he hides behind his kids and his estranged wife (or his job). He's full of excuses as to why he can't get serious "at this point in time." He says he "just hasn't had time" to file for divorce, though he has been separated for seven years.

The Substance Abuser

He's hyper; he talks a lot; his nose is usually running. (Or: He drinks too many cocktails before dinner, too much wine with dinner, and too many nightcaps after dinner.) You *should* be committed if you want to settle down with him.

The Boldly Unavailable

He admits he's married, and says that he and his wife stay together only for the sake of the kids. He and his spouse don't communicate and haven't slept together for years. If you get involved with him, he may ask you to be patient. Instead, get smart and get out.

The Conqueror
He's interested only in the chase; he finds a healthy monogamous relationship boring. At the end of the evening, he assumes you'll consent to a sexual encounter. If you decline the invitation, he'll think there is something clinically wrong with you, and will probably share his insights. If you *don't* decline, you may learn that he's a great lover. He gets a lot of practice. He will continue to do so—with other women.

The Egomaniac
He's flashy and totally self-consumed. He gets regular manicures; he may be in the process of a hair transplant. If you let him talk about himself all night, he'll conclude that you're a great conversationalist. His only commitment is to his image. (You'd have to fight for mirror space, anyway.)

The Mama's Boy
Unusually devoted to his mother, he spends more nights with her than with you. He talks to her daily, pays her rent, and buys her cars. He's simply never been weaned; there's no room for you. (Good luck in eliciting his support if you ever have a disagreement with his mother!)

God

He is committed to a Greater Cause and is Very Important in his field. You'd have to walk three steps behind him. He won't pay attention to you long enough to commit.

The Adolescent

A great guy, fun to be with, outgoing—but his favorite topics of conversation all have to do with high school and/or college and/or the old fraternity brothers. He's stuck in adolescence. He says he'll recognize the right person "when the bells go off"; in fact, he's waiting for the romantic intensity and infatuation of youthful loves to return. Don't wait with him.

The Collector

Quantity, not quality, is the issue as far as this fellow's relationships go. Women are babes, chicks, girls, foxes, cupcakes, pumpkins, or any other name that can turn a human being into an animal or object. He'll never take you seriously. Get away quickly.

The Chronic Underachiever

A professional student, he has several master's degrees; he's still in graduate school at age 40. He may still live in his parents' home. He is a well-read, walking void you will be unable to fill.

The Homosexual

You were probably introduced by overly optimistic friends. Rule Number One: If you cannot meet each other's needs, move on.

The Do-Gooder

He's caught up in every big cause—peace, the homeless, Save the Planet. All his time and energy are devoted to huge issues that he is, for all his good intentions, ultimately not responsible for. He cannot commit on a personal and intimate level. Unless you have a thing about one-night stands in sleeping bags, forget it.

The Woman Hater

The less said about this gentleman, the better. See your well-thumbed copy of *The Bell Jar* if you need a refresher course. Exit immediately.

The Dependent

He's looking for someone to take care of him or his kids. (In older men, health can be an issue.) Ask yourself what makes it a relationship.

● ● ●

"BUT I CAN CHANGE HIM!"

It's been said that women are constantly trying to change the emotional environment, trying to make it better, trying to find a higher standard, trying to figure it out. That may be true. You may be able to make both your mate and yourself better people. But if your intended bears a strong resemblance to any of the profiles above, step back and count to ten.

No, the list does not rule out every man—just the ones with the obvious, potentially catastrophic drawbacks. Go over the list a few times, then decide for yourself. If your man is idiosyncratic, bordering on bizarre, or just a creep, look elsewhere.

Profile of A Noncommitter

Michael: aged 44; divorced for twelve years; three children. Occupation—salesman.

I want to tell you exactly why I will never commit. I am the leader of the boys. I am the role model; someone recently called me the only truly free man he knows.

I was married for eight years. I always think that if I wanted to be married, I would have stayed married. I left because I didn't want to be married; I didn't like the institution. I enjoyed the fact that I had children; I like my children, and I've always supported them, but I have no desire to be married.

I like the company of women, but I like variety. I don't like to be pinned down. My life-

style is such that I don't need women for financial support; I'm successful financially. I travel all the time and I like to travel alone. I like my business and that also involves a great deal of travel and meeting a lot of different people. I always seem to have one major girlfriend and then other like . . . friends. At times I think I'm in love, and it's fun; it's that initial feeling, but it never really lasts. I don't really know what love is other than sexual love.

I don't believe in marriage, other than to have kids. I don't see too many successful marriages, and I don't think it's something that a person needs. To me, the reasons that a lot of the people stay married are the wrong reasons; they stay for the children or because they can't afford to leave.

Once you're divorced, I think you become bitter about the institution of marriage, because if you're a man, it costs you a lot of money. In the first couple of years after I was divorced, I had very little money. I think there's just a little too much dependence in marriage; women become controlling and they want to run parts of your life that they think you haven't been successful at. Almost every woman I've had a relationship with has given me an ultimatum, and we end up breaking up.

I tell the women I date that I'm not interested in marriage. Some believe me but most

*don't; they think that I'm going to change at
some point.*

● ● ●

Let's face it; this is an unusually candid expression of
a mindset that is not uncommon among some men.
Don't make mistakes with a person like this. Your love
can't cure this guy, and it's flat-out useless to try to
force him into a situation that he is essentially un-
suited for. Move on.

CHAPTER FOUR

The Committer vs. The Noncommitter

A guide to recognizing the real thing.

"I'll call."
— The Noncommitter

THE CONNECTION

The committer.
If he's serious about a relationship, he'll be more in-clined to ask friends, relatives, and people he works with for introductions; he'll probably be open to blind dates. He may even go to a dating service—presumably everybody is there for the same reason. He knows that a woman may not take him seriously if they meet in a bar or under other circumstances that may make her feel uneasy about the encounter.

The noncommitter.
He's always looking for *women*—not a woman. There's

no room in his life for a permanent woman; he's into cruising. He's usually active in the bar scene. Society and his family put pressure on him to "settle down," so he has a lot of excuses about why he can't find the right woman. He's an expert at avoiding the possibilities.

LET'S TALK

The committer.
He asks questions, he listens, he remembers things. He pays attention. You don't feel like you're starting over again with every date. He doesn't give evasive answers to innocuous questions. He's at ease with himself; he talks openly about his past. He's willing to meet your friends, family, and parents—and to introduce you to his.

The noncommitter.
He is usually supporting too many other things (or people). You're the one who has to listen.

WARDROBE

The committer.
He usually dresses neatly, casually, and fairly conservatively. He's less likely to wear a jacket and tie on a regular basis than the noncommitter. He may well need your help in this area. Don't be surprised to see:

> Soft colored golf shirts without logos
> Oxford cloth cotton button-down shirts
> Khaki pants

Sports coat
Boat shoes
Tube socks
Boxer shorts
Dockers (anything)

The noncommitter:
He wears more jewelry than you do. His nails are manicured. His hair is carefully styled. He wears designer clothing. Everything is slick and smooth, and he wants it to stay that way. He doesn't need you. Don't be surprised to see:

Diamond pinky rings
Fitted dress shirts
Silk pajamas or robe
Bally shoes
Slip-on loafers or running shoes (he's ready
    for a quick getaway)
Tank tops
Bikini underwear
Camel's hair coat (not the attire of someone
    who plans to lift small children)
Armani (anything)

CAREERS

The committer:
He has a job where he is readily available and able to meet the needs of others. Likely to be a:

Fireman
Schoolteacher

Funeral director
Attorney
Missionary
Computer programmer
Stock analyst
Banker
Construction worker
Minister
Politician

The noncommitter.
Likely to be a:

Surgeon
Actor
Commercial photographer (too many models
    available)
Writer (subject to abject poverty and depres-
    sion)
Lumberjack
Pilot
Traveling salesman
Politician (they make both lists; they're two-
    faced)

WORDS

The committer.
He formalizes plans. He'll say, "Let's have dinner Wednesday" or "I'll call you tomorrow afternoon."

The noncommitter.
He always leaves you with an uncomfortable feeling; things are always up in the air. You'll always be wondering: Are we doing something next week? Will he call? What he does say sounds like a line; he may yell something over his shoulder in passing like, "I'll call" or "Talk to you soon." (He may try to "date" by telephone; he'll call and say, "I can't wait to see you" or "Your body makes me crazy." You wonder if you're on a checklist of some sort.)

THE DRIVING FORCE

The committer.
He drives station wagons, Jeeps, Volvos, old cars with sentimental value, and Japanese cars because they're a good value and last a long time.

The noncommitter.
He's obvious. He drives a penis extension car: Trans Am, Corvette, BMW, Porsche. In everything he does, he's trying to make a strong statement. He usually succeeds.

ANIMAL MAGNETISM

The committer.
He may have a dog; it shows that he's interested in companionship. (Dogs require a great deal of work.)

The noncommitter.
Expect extremes. He may not have time for another

living being; or he may be weird about his pets. One fellow I heard of gave his parrots their own bedroom and called them his little girls. He fed them from his plate and gave them gin and tonic from a glass. His long-term commitment was obviously toward his feathered friends.

HOME LIFE

The committer:
His apartment is probably not decorated well. Things may stay in boxes for too long. Light bulbs may hang unadorned from the ceiling. He's waiting for a woman to help get things in order.

The noncommitter:
Nice place. Probably professionally decorated. See the *House and Garden* magazines on the coffee table? Notice the color scheme: black, gray, and white. His home has lots of sharp edges. It is technically impressive, but ultimately cold. Women are not meant to live here.

THE GREAT GETAWAY

The committer:
He says he's usually too busy for vacations, but the truth is he doesn't want to go alone. When he can fit it in, he goes to:

> Disney World
> Family reunions
> Canada for fishing trips with buddies

Spas or camps specifically designed to provide the opportunity to meet women with
a similar interest (tennis camp, writers'
colony, hiking club)

The noncommitter.
He goes to:

Club Med
The wine country of France
High school reunions
The Greek Islands
The Olympics
Oktoberfest (lots of crowds, some parties,
some sex, then you're gone)
Windjammer cruises (ditto, once you pull
into port)
Rio (home of the thong bathing suit)

SPORTS

The committer.
He participates in team sports: baseball, football, bas-
ketball. He likes boating and fishing.

The noncommitter.
He won't join a team sport. He wants to do what he
feels like when he feels like it. He's involved in solo
sports that won't require anything that pins him down:
windsurfing, jogging, swimming, golfing.

MOVIES
The committer.
His favorite movies:

> *It's a Wonderful Life*
> Anything from the Disney studios, 1934-
> 1955
> *Dark Victory* (He's a sucker for Bette Davis)
> Kevin Costner's *Robin Hood* (he's not self-
> centered and admires the story's
> altruism)
> Rocky and Bullwinkle cartoons (they're a loyal
> pair and have been together forever)

The noncommitter.
His real hero is James Bond. Other favorites include:

> Anything featuring Clint, Sly, or Arnold
> Roadrunner cartoons (the hero always gets
> away)

THE LIBRARY
The committer.
Loves books of many kinds.

The noncommitter.
He may *have* books, but don't be fooled; ask him which ones he's read lately. In fact, he sticks to magazines; he's not ready to make the commitment to a whole book. He's read one article about a woman's issue and considers himself an expert.

THE DATE

The committer:

He's polite, keeps eye contact, and will not bring up the subject of money when you go to the restaurant. He's not concerned with contrived or overwhelming events (big parties, clubs, large groups) where you have little or no opportunity to get to know one another. He's more interested in being with you than in any particular setting. He's levelheaded enough to start off with a movie and dinner. He's willing to have dinner at your place; he appreciates good cooking. Your company is enough to sustain him; it's clear he wants to get to know you. At the end of the date, he's likely to want to set another one, with specific whens and wheres.

The noncommitter:

He's not really interested in getting to know you, so you won't find yourself in many situations where one-on-one conversations can occur. He goes where he can be seen, and he wants to see what else is out there. He'll order the wine without consulting you and/or order trendy food (such as sushi) that is calculated to impress. When he does talk, he monopolizes the conversation. He usually manages to steer things back toward the topics of sex and money. He dresses better than you do. He may sport an earring. You know less about him at the end of the night than you did at the beginning.

SEX

The committer:

He may be disappointed, but he will not react angrily

or immaturely if you want to take things slowly and put off sleeping with him. If you do decide to go to bed together, he will want to hang around the next morning and have breakfast. He needs time with you before dashing away. He needs to decompress, just like you do.

The noncommitter.
He generally will not stay the whole night or invite you to. If he does stay, he will not want breakfast. He may not even remove his socks or wristwatch during sex. He makes you feel like he's not really there. And he isn't.

CHAPTER FIVE

Finding Romance

*"I knew there was no way
they could conduct
themselves that way in
their business lives."*

— Bob

If you wait passively for love to happen, you may bump into your mate in the course of your daily routine . . . or you may find yourself waiting forever.

In romance you must take the initiative in discovering eligible men rather than leaving the matter up to chance. After all, you want to get married—too important an objective for you not to take an active role in its completion.

You won't meet a man by staying at home, so you

must get out. Enroll in courses of interest, accept invitations, and take risks. Be on the lookout and be alert; eligible men are everywhere—the office, business meetings, the supermarket, even the fellow sitting next to you on the plane. Your friends and family members can act as your representatives, keeping an eye out for you. Dating services and personals ads can also be effective ways of meeting men. An excellent way of finding a man with interests similar to yours is by joining a club or organization that focuses on your hobbies, interests, or sports activities.

At the same time, don't let yourself believe that marriage is all there is to life. You're a person in your own right, and if you're consumed with anxiety about finding a mate, your desperation will scare off even the most willing to commit. Believe in yourself, and others will be drawn to you naturally.

● ● ●

There are many ways of meeting eligible men, but the following story illustrates how not to.

Kathy was driving home from work one evening when a car pulled up beside her. The male driver waved her over to the side of the road. "I thought he was cute and I'd had a glass of wine, so I stopped to meet him," she recalled later. "We got out of our cars and started to talk, and he asked me to dinner. That's how it began."

Kathy couldn't understand when Don turned out

to be so unreliable; she later learned that the way she met Don was his *modus operandi* for meeting women, one that he continued to use even after they began to date.

She was lucky he didn't turn out to be dangerous. The chances of a serious or permanent relationship developing out of a meeting such as this are slim to none. You're usually better off following the more conventional methods of meeting a man.

THE ELIMINATION PROCESS

During the selection/elimination process, you will seek out the available men and weed out the undesirables through a screening process.

You're not after just any man; you're after a specific type, your ideal, someone who reflects your taste in men. You can significantly narrow down the number by imposing your individual restrictions. For example, what qualities would you like your future spouse to have? Eliminate all men who do not meet your criteria and concentrate on those who do. Look at a man not only as a prospective date but also as a future husband. Don't eliminate candidates on the basis of superficial or unimportant considerations such as height or appearance, but do consider the following:

● Is he a stable candidate of good moral character?

● Does he need and desire a permanent relationship?

● Are you his type?

- Can you satisfy his primary and secondary commitment factors?

  (*Primary:* Companionship, love, sexual fulfillment)

  (*Secondary:* Sense of humor, emotional stability, appearance on your own terms and esthetic)

- Can he satisfy your needs?

● ● ●

Look for honest, reliable men, and never concentrate on just one fellow in the beginning stages. Keep your options open. Cultivate friendships with many men who appeal to you and who respond to your overtures of friendship. You can spend a lot of time with one man, but not give up the others until you're relatively certain a commitment will be forthcoming.

In some ways, looking for a man is a lot like looking for a job. For instance, it is generally easier to find a job when you're employed than when you're not. A desperate woman with no other option is extremely unattractive, and more than one man who responded to the survey spoke of being able to sense such a woman "a mile away." If you fall into this category, you are not in a great bargaining position.

MEN NEED, TOO

A *need* is defined as "a condition or situation in which

something necessary or desirable is required or wanted; a wish for something that is lacking or desired; a necessity."

In romance, you will be happy to learn, the cards are stacked in your favor. Statistically, of the four population groups—married men, single men, married women, single women—*single men rank as the most unhappy.*

According to a recent article by Morton Hunt in *Longevity Magazine*, getting married pays off—in lifespan—for men.

> *Only a spouse will do, at least for men, according to a new study reported at a recent meeting of the American Public Health Association. Epidemiologist Maradee Davis, Ph.D., and three co-researchers at the University of California, San Francisco (UCSF) analyzed data from the National Health and Nutrition Examination Survey conducted by the National Center for Health Statistics. Their findings: unmarried men between the ages of 45 and 64, regardless of whether they lived alone or with someone else, were twice as likely to die within ten years as were married men in that age range. "Both men who live alone and those who live with someone other than a spouse are equally disadvantaged for survival," says Davis. "The critical factor seems to be the presence of a spouse."*

If that's not a need, nothing is. What's more, men

know it. Men sense the inadequacy of living without a woman in their lives, though they are not always able to articulate it clearly. At root, however, most of them know that there is a powerful truth behind the traditional notion of a man being somehow incomplete without a wife.

WOMEN MEN WON'T COMMIT TO

Just as we examined warning signals you should watch out for when seeking a mate, we should be aware that women can also possess negative traits that can send men running in the opposite direction. Now is the time for a little honest self-appraisal.

Attitude heads the list here. Listen to what Bob, a 34-year-old media executive, had to say on the subject:

> *"There is one thing I simply would not put up with, and that was whining. I ran into more women who were attractive, established professionals, but who simply had a terrible attitude when it came to talking to men on a social level. I knew there was no way they could conduct themselves that way in their business lives, and it made me feel like a second-class encounter that they would spend an hour or two whining at me or talking themselves down."*

As mentioned earlier, it is imperative that you avoid negative people and emotions. Whiners congregate with whiners!

Are you presenting as many positive signals as possible? Are you demonstrating that you are able to meet the needs of the man you are looking for? Be realistic. Don't castigate yourself if you run into trouble; give yourself time. You may need to re-evaluate the means by which you will attain your goal(s), or the schedule you committed to.

Now then: about appearance. Research has shown that married couples tend to be of the same level of attractiveness; that is, gorgeous women often end up with extremely handsome men. Conversely, very unattractive women tend to end up with men who are not very good-looking, either. It follows that if you want to attract a hunk, you will have to become a female counterpart of that level of attractiveness. Fortunately, this can, in many cases, have little to do with the looks you're born with. Attractiveness—which I would distinguish from physical beauty—has to do with style, dressing well, broadcasting confidence, being alluring.

Initially, it may be necessary to rethink the whole male-female concept. It's not man-woman any longer, but people-people. Bear that in mind, and get rid of any old baggage—especially (and this warrants repetition) angers from past relationships before you embark on your new life. You will soon find someone to share it with.

CHAPTER SIX

The Dos and Don'ts of Seduction

"Sensual is better than sexy."

— Mark

Is that elusive quality we call "the right chemistry" truly spontaneous . . . or can you help it to develop? I believe you can learn to send out sensual vibrations, thereby creating a magical romantic pull. And I believe we have more control over "chemistry" than most people would imagine.

When you have met a man to whom you are attracted, there are subtle behavioral patterns you can employ that can help bring about the feeling of "rightness" about the relationship for a man. This "rightness" may be as close as we can come to defining that ineluctable factor known as love, which was among the most common responses men gave to explain their decision to commit. After all, "falling in love" is a process with certain distinct features—and in the beginning stages, it is up to you to exude the femininity and sensuality that will make him want to bond with you.

Bear in mind that you—and all of us—continually send out signals without meaning to through facial and body expressions, as well as in conversation. It's part of our animal nature. Learn to recognize the signals your body is sending and go with them; after the primary attraction takes hold, the other elements (intellectual compatibility, mutual emotional support, and so on) can take hold and develop. But you must help to initiate that primary chemistry. Here are some specific ideas on how you can do that.

THE DOS
DO be aware of your sexuality and how to use it.
DO practice direct eye contact.

> *"Sensual is better than sexy; it's more subtle. It could mean a gesture or the way she smiles. Deirdre is sensual. Whenever I'm around her, I can feel this tingling warmth. I can feel it flowing from her body to mine. I think other people around us can also sense it. She was different than other women; she makes me feel special like no one ever did. She pays attention to me when I talk . . . she always looks*

*me in the eye and parts her lips a little bit. It's
enticing."* (Mark, a 33-year-old dentist.)

DO be mysterious.
DO be provocative.

*"I'd rather be fooled a little bit in the begin-
ning. But for the relationship to last, it has to
have depth. It all has to do with the fantasy
. . . if she isn't interesting and doesn't have
her own life, then nothing will happen."*
(Josh, a 52-year-old accountant.)

DO put your best image forward.
DO project an air of confidence.
DO be independent.

*"I didn't want to be a caretaker. I need the
stimulation that Johanna brings to our
relationship. That comes from her commitment
to her career as well as her independence. She
does her own thing and she knows how to
handle money. I don't like dependent women.
They remind me of my first wife. I would never
have married Johanna if she were not her own
person with her own life."* (Thomas, a 37-year-
old computer programmer.)

DO join an exercise club and get in shape, but DON'T
get into bodybuilding.

"Physical (attractiveness) is important to me,

> *but that doesn't necessarily mean attributes a*
> *woman is born with. Any reasonably attrac-*
> *tive woman can be sensual if she has nice*
> *hair and smooth skin and she stays in*
> *shape."* (Seth, a 47-year-old advertising ex-
> ecutive.)

DO let your hair grow. (One man told me that
short-haired women reminded him of dowdy, middle-
aged real estate agents.)

DO learn to accentuate your mouth and eyes in
a soft and subtle way. Less is better, and the clown
look is out.

> *"I like women who are soft and natural. Make-*
> *up, in general, I don't like. I like flowing hair. I*
> *like women who wear sweeping dresses . . . .*
> *I was introduced to this woman who wore a*
> *great deal of make-up and had her hair all*
> *done; she had this 'I-want-to-be-a-housewife'*
> *look about her. That's not me."* (Adam, a 26-
> year-old writer.)

DO learn how to be a sensual kisser.
DO wear perfume.

> *"What turns me on? Perfume. It makes my head*
> *dizzy, brings out the primate in me . . . I like*
> *sexy dressing if it's done right. For instance, a*
> *skirt with a deep slit, rather than a very short*
> *skirt.' It's much more seductive. Oh, yes, and*

sandals on bare feet." (Ken, a 48-year-old operations manager.)

DO act like a female. (After all, that's what you're lucky enough to be.)
DO flirt.

"I hate blatantly aggressive women . . . I suppose I want to think I'm calling the shots. I figure if she comes on to me like that, she probably does with a lot of guys. My wife Jean didn't chase me, although she was a flirt, and I like that. The way she smiled at me and looked at me and paid attention to what I said. I could tell she was turned on by me. But she didn't say, 'When are we going out?' or 'Come on over to my house,' or 'Let's go to bed.' I had the fun of working up to it. To think about it." (Brent, a 38-year-old designer.)

DO be an interesting conversationalist and a good communicator.
DO be sensitive to the needs of others.

"I knew almost from the beginning that I wanted to marry Elizabeth. She wasn't the best-looking woman I ever dated, but she was feminine and articulate and smart and well dressed. A great conversationalist. She was genuinely interested in other people. There was a nurturing side to her that had been lacking in other women. She was also very

bright and her wit was intriguing. I couldn't wait for my parents to meet her." (Kevin, a 27-year-old architect.)

DO have a drink if you're so inclined, but DON'T get drunk.

"A woman who drinks too much scares me . . . (Drinking too much) is a symptom of other, greater problems, an unhappiness or inability to deal with life on a real level. It's not smart and it's very unattractive." (Les, a 38-year-old salesman.)

DO take classes in cooking and specialize in seductive suppers for two. (Besides having fun and learning something exciting, you could meet some interesting men.)

DO realize how effective your voice can be.

"When I was about fourteen, I saw Lauren Bacall in the movie To Have and Have Not. *I fell in love. Linda has that same sultry, husky voice. I'm frequently out of town on business, and when I call Linda, I melt when I hear her on the phone."* (Christopher, a 33-year-old sales manager.)

THE DON'TS

DON'T bare your soul too soon.

> *"I love the whole process of getting to know a woman gradually . . . wondering and anticipating what will happen next. If I had one piece of advice to pass along to women, it would be, 'Don't tell him everything on the first date.' It comes across as a form of desperation. I'm interested in having fun; I don't want to feel like a father confessor. If I already know everything about her, it feels like there's no reason to see her again."* (Jack, a 41-year-old graphic artist.)

DON'T be vulgar or make a habit of swearing.
DON'T chew gum or spit.
DON'T dress like a man.
DON'T be a male-basher.
DON'T carry a chip on your shoulder from past relationships that didn't work out.
DON'T give the impression you're vain, rude, or self-absorbed.

> *"I'd meet an attractive woman; we start to talk and suddenly I realize her eyes are darting behind me to see what else is going on in the room. Nothing turns me off more. It's a real insult. Or she's preoccupied with her hair or something, constantly checking the mirror. Just rude behavior. She could be absolutely*

gorgeous and I'd never call her again." (Neil, a 37-year-old pilot.)

DON'T smoke. (It may take willpower to quit, but do it anyway. More and more men are declining the invitation to spend the rest of their lives with someone who smells like an ashtray.)

DON'T tell a man you've just met that you're looking for a husband.

> *"Desperation scares the hell out of me. Call me a hopeless romantic, but broadcasting that you're getting married because you're running out of time is cold and calculating, and it's not my idea of the best way to start a relationship."* (Clark, a 33-year-old engineer.)

DON'T be a fashion victim.

> *"Martha doesn't have the greatest figure; she's a little overweight, but she always looks great because she knows what suits her. She doesn't go along with the latest trends if they don't flatter her. And she carries herself sort of regally . . . she's got great posture. You can't help but notice when she comes into the room. She's sexy and beautiful and I'm very proud of her."* (Blaine, a 43-year-old consultant.)

DON'T speak cruelly about other people behind their backs. (Your man may wonder what you'll say about him when he's not around.)

● ● ●

While many men may express a preconceived ideal or a preference for a particular body type or hair color, the overwhelming majority are not foolish enough to rule out every woman who does not fit within the category. It only takes one attractive, seductive woman to change what makes for a "perfect woman"—and get "the right chemistry" to kick in.

As Gary, a 43-year-old attorney said,

"If I had to answer what type of woman I'm attracted to, I would say without hesitation that she should be 5' 6' or under and fairly slender. But then I'd also have to admit that the woman I'm currently involved with is six feet tall and on the robust side. What attracted me was her conversation, her personality, the jokes we shared. I guess it was more of an intangible thing having to do with personality and interaction in the long run."

DO be yourself and the best you can be. You'll find there's someone out there who will love you and commit to you for what you are.

STRATEGIES FOR MAKING YOURSELF LOVABLE

You will attract a man and make yourself indispensable by figuring out how best to satisfy his needs. The bulk of this book is meant to show you how to identify those needs; right now, however, we must take some time to focus on creative strategies for presenting yourself as the attractive, available, and lovable potential mate that you really are. You are going to examine, develop, and enhance yourself, with an eye toward eventually targeting the needs of the men you find interesting. And you are going to start by getting to know *you.*

You've heard it before, but it really is essential: You must know who you are before you can hope to begin a mutually fulfilling intimate relationship. You must develop your own personality before you invest massive amounts of time and energy looking for a potential mate. You must learn how to develop the qualities and characteristics of a complete, confident, independent individual. You must, in short, become a winner in your own eyes.

Here are some ideas on how to start doing just that.

WORK FROM A POSITIVE STATE OF MIND; SMILE GENUINELY WHENEVER YOU CAN.

Smiles are infectious when they are unforced. Remember that facial expressions (positive or negative) are a form of body language that reveal your inner self.

AVOID NEGATIVE PEOPLE AND EMOTIONS.

Make a list of the people you surround yourself with. Cross off the whiners, the ones who lament, "I always seem to end up with married men" or "All the good ones are taken." They drag you down—and they broadcast false messages. (Remember that many good men come up for "recycling" periodically.) Is "dropping a friend" too cruel a step? It may seem harsh, but you must put your own goals first, and that means that you simply cannot afford to surround yourself with negative people.

BEGIN YOUR OWN PERSONAL SELF-ANALYSIS.

Are you the best person you can be? Don't set unrealistic goals; make yourself your own special long-term project. Research indicates that if you want to attract an extremely attractive man, you will need to project a similar level of attractiveness. Fortunately, this has little to do with the looks you're born with; it has to do with style, dressing well, broadcasting confidence, being alluring. For many women, going on a weight-loss program is an excellent way to start; there are dozens of other ways to work on becoming the best you imaginable. Remember that, ultimately, you are doing what you do for yourself first—not for someone else's approval.

GET RID OF OLD BAGGAGE.

You will probably have to work through any angers from past relationships before embarking on your new life. Start with a clean slate; muster all your positive energy to achieve your goal. You are now looking for a companion and a best friend as well as a lover, so your attitude should be warm and trusting, not combative.

MAKE SPECIFIC GOALS AND SET TIME LIMITS FOR SELF-IMPROVEMENT.

Record everything in a notebook; refer to it constantly. You must accept, integrate, and be intimately familiar with your goals. If you think that people don't respect you intellectually, examine the reasons and take steps to turn the situation around. Enroll in a few courses or find out how you can complete an undergraduate degree if you haven't done so.

LEARN MORE ABOUT THE WORLD AROUND YOU.

If you don't already, make a habit of reading the newspaper daily. Become more aware of local, national, and world events. You may want to start out with the objective of finding one area in which you have an extremely uncommon or unconventional view—that will help keep conversations rolling!

TEAM UP.

If it's easier for you to go to the YWCA as part of a group, do it. (You can also join a health club with a friend or two, but this is more expensive.) With a companion or two, you can count on your friends to encourage you to stick with it even on days when you don't feel like sticking to your goal.

MAKE AN EFFORT TO LOOK MORE FEMININE.

Your office attire, for instance. Wear clothes that flatter and accentuate your positives; don't settle for a drab look. You want to look like a professional, yes, but there's no law that says you have to fade into the background in doing so. And what about a new hairdo more often—just to liven things up? Everybody needs a change now and then. Finally, consider going to the cosmetic section of a department store and having a professional makeover done. It usually doesn't cost anything, although you may want to purchase some of the items applied. Most of the good cosmetic companies (such as Clinique, Lancome, Estee Lauder and others) will have skilled personnel on hand who are eager to show what their products can do for you.

MOVING AHEAD

You are your own ongoing project; the person who greets you in the mirror each morning is full of potential, but she must keep striving, keep looking for challenges, keep moving forward. Becoming a better you is an ongoing process, not an isolated event. (There is a Zen saying that goes, "Even the Buddha has not stopped working on himself.")

CHAPTER SEVEN

The Commitment

"I've figured men out."
— Ruth

Your goal is to motivate a man to propose or accept a proposal of marriage.

Let's look at things from your man's viewpoint for a moment. He will not want to commit to anyone other than the best wife he can find, a woman he will want to have at his side for life. A long-term relationship begins with the compatibility of your personality and his; it starts in a casual way and is built on trust. You must be honest and straightforward, and you must convince him that you are the best woman he has ever dated. This is probably the biggest step he's ever going to make, and he wants to do it right.

Consider this telling comment from Chris, a 32-year-old attorney:

> *"Suzanne filled all the gaps; she was right where everyone else had been wrong. I knew I couldn't afford to let her slip through my hands."*

Chris's observation offers some illuminating insights on the way men's minds work. Note how easily Chris makes the transition from Suzanne's having been "right where everyone else was wrong" to Suzanne's becoming the kind of woman he couldn't let "slip through" his hands. Generally speaking, I have found that once a man enters the mindset of considering looking seriously for a mate, the task ahead of the woman becomes quite clear-cut. (Not necessarily *easy*, mind you, but clear-cut.) You will win your chosen man by *fulfilling a need or needs that have not been met in his former intimate relationships.*

"WHAT'S IN IT FOR ME?"

Let's be honest. Everyone in the wonderful world of dating is motivated by the WIIFM? (What's In It for Me?) concept. No man is going to make the ultimate commitment without getting something he feels he needs in return.

Some men don't require much convincing when it comes to the concept of marriage. As one 50-year-old dentist put it,

> *"It felt right to be married. I needed the sense of family. My parents and grandparents were happily married."*

A divorced physician expressed it another way.

> *"In my profession, it's impractical and socially awkward not to be married. I didn't like going to a medical conference and introducing a woman as 'my friend.' "*

If you're trying to get a man to commit, you've got to think about what your man is looking for. Every man, like every woman, has a list of needs and desires. This list has developed over the course of a lifetime and reflects both intrinsic characteristics and influences from upbringing and experience. One man could be looking for a woman with enough money to enhance his lifestyle; another might want someone to fulfill the role of mother for his children. In such a case, his concept of a "good wife" could well depend on what he grew up with—what was *his* mother like?

According to Doris Lilly, author of the 1951 book *How to Marry a Millionaire*, "The wives pack for them, make their phone calls, and see that their drawers look nice. It's intoxicating for a man to be waited on. Combine this with very skillful sex, and that will get them."

What Lilly is really talking about here is making your man comfortable, fitting into his life in such a way that he'd feel bereft without you.

● ● ●

One December a few years back, after a recent breakup with a man I'd been dating for several months, I was Christmas shopping for my son in the men's section of a large department store. The middle-aged saleswoman, whose name was Ruth, asked if I was buying a gift for my husband. I explained that I was single; before long, I found myself sharing the entire story of my failed relationship. Ruth, herself newly divorced, listened attentively and offered advice; the surrounding women shoppers listened with growing interest.

> *"I've figured men out,"* she said. *"I know what they want. Be lovely, witty, charming; give them their space and feed them. My mother-in-law used to say that all you had to do to keep a man happy was treat him like a dog—feed him and pet him. I know a way to cook brisket your fellow will die for."*

With these words, she wrote down her recipe on my sales slip and carefully pressed it into the palm of my hand.

She came from a different generation, yes, but there was truth to her advice. Put into terms we may be able to understand better today, she was advising me to show conscientious caretaking.

MARRIAGE BENEFITS

As a prospective wife, you're offering to undertake a lifetime change, one of the most important adjustments you or the man will ever make. It's up to you to know how to make his life more enjoyable and less problematic. This offer must be made clear in your behavior toward him, in words and deeds that enhance the quality of his life.

This should be done with careful planning, because if he's dating other women and is ready to commit but hasn't settled on a particular woman, he may end up with another female who presents herself as capable of being a better wife. Put more bluntly, you may have competition.

Here are a few tips to enhance your chances for success.

THE SUCCESS FORMULA

STEP ONE.

After you've decided on the man you want to marry, listen and observe him carefully. What does he consider to be his primary needs? What does he feel was missing in his past relationships? Let him know how much you have in common. Without changing your personality, make sure he realizes that you represent the best "fit." For instance, if he's an avid baseball fan, you might familiarize yourself with the sport—or surprise him with a gift of tickets so you and he can attend a game together. To really impress him, try tossing this out: "Bob Gibson's '68 season will never be matched in my book. To win twenty and post an ERA of 1.12; that's ridiculous. I'll take Gibby and those Cards over Ryan, Clemens, Seaver—anyone." Of course, you should be able to stand up under questioning.

A devoted father would appreciate the freedom to discuss his children with you and possibly even spend time with all of you together. If he's crazy about meatloaf, learn how to make the best meatloaf dinner he's ever had. Find his needs as he defines them—then fill them.

STEP TWO.

Don't change your personal goals. Mature, confident men respect an independent woman who has her own life and interests. Intimacy and independence can go hand in hand.

STEP THREE.

Let him pursue you. Men still like to think of themselves as the hunters. Don't make them relinquish control; guide them. Think of yourself entering a store; an aggressive salesperson instantly approaches you and inquires, "May I help you?" You back off, but the salesperson continues to hover, making you feel uncomfortable and trapped. "Looking for something special?" the person persists. You feel anxious, perhaps even afraid, and reply, "I'm just looking, thanks." Then, more likely than not, you leave without making a purchase. Now consider the low-key approach: "Hi, my name is Barbara. If I can be of any help, please let me know." This leaves you feeling relaxed, unthreatened, in a mood to shop. In romance, the same principle applies. In most cases, if you use high-pressure tactics, he'll back off.

STEP FOUR.

Remember that every man wants an enabler. By being supportive of his ideas and dreams, by being a nurturer and a good listener, you enable him to put his best foot forward. Supply him with opportunities to make things happen by encouraging him to talk about his goals and plans. Share the small details in his life. Embrace him warmly as a partner in whom you feel genuine confidence.

STEP FIVE.

Don't be afraid to compliment him in every area in which he excels—sexuality, appearance, talent, or personality. It is a rare man indeed who does not enjoy being admired by a woman; it adds to his self-confidence. Learn to turn negatives into positives: If you don't like his clothing, give him a shirt you do like and tell him how sexy he looks in it. *Don't* tell him he has "no idea how to dress properly."

STEP SIX.

Don't share too much too soon. Telling "war stories" about former lovers has a negative impact in the early stages of a relationship. Leave the excess baggage behind. No man wants an angry woman with an axe to grind over past hurts. (There is also the distinct possibility that he will begin to wonder what a man who decided to leave you knew that he doesn't.) Other than morbid curiosity, there is simply no reason to pry into his past or tell him about yours at the outset of your relationship. If he asks about your first marriage or last partner, smile sweetly and say, "I'm having such a good time right now, I'd rather not talk about it." Practice saying this aloud in front of a mirror if you have to.

STEP SEVEN.

Surprise him by sending him flowers or buying a little gift for no particular reason. Put a picture of yourself in his wallet or briefcase so he'll have the opportunity to think of you when you're not with him.

STEP EIGHT.

Hone your sensory skills. People often make a decision based on their feelings rather than entirely on logic, and men are no exception. Until he gets that wholly positive feeling about marrying you, he won't commit. A touch, a song, a gesture, or a fragrance might remind him of you and might cause him to miss you and want to be with you. He may make a decision to commit based on that sensory feeling. Even if he takes a more hard-nosed approach, your man *must* be emotionally close before he'll propose; music, scent, and other sensory charms will help.

STEP NINE.

Don't feel pressured into an early sexual encounter. Get to know him first. For one thing, casual sex is just too dangerous these days; for another, you want to be sure that things are progressing steadily, not in a dash. Keep the relationship at your speed—and stay away from the stormy pace at which men often would like to see things move ahead. If he's truly interested in you, he will wait to have sex until the timing is right for you and an emotional connection has taken place. Slowing down in this way reduces the chances of your getting hurt emotionally and allows the man to remain in the "hunt" stage. Whatever you do, don't attempt to use sex as a quick way to solidify the relationship or "trap" the man—this virtually always backfires. (It's interesting to note that the 25-to-35-year-old men I interviewed claimed near-unanimous preference for an "experienced virgin" as a marriage partner—whatever that is. Note, too, that there is still a certain stigma surrounding a woman who is an avowed veteran of numerous sexual campaigns. Of course, no such stigma exists for men.)

STEP TEN.

If sex does enter the picture, relax and enjoy yourself. Men appreciate a good lover who enjoys her own sexuality. After your relationship has deepened naturally to the point at which making love will be an honest expression of how you feel toward each other, make an effort to set off some real fireworks. Try to get hold of a copy of *The Sensuous Woman*, by "J". It's essential reading, and tells you things your mother probably should have, but never did (such as how to perform oral sex competently). Your man will soon be inclined to seek sexual satisfaction in the only sensible manner: with you.

STEP ELEVEN.

Invest in pretty, high-quality underwear and a couple of sexy nightgowns. How do you think your lover would want you to look in bed? Most men aren't aroused by women who wear granny gowns or T-shirts and slouch socks as nightclothes.

STEP TWELVE.

Build a nest. Make him feel comfortable in your home from the beginning of your dating. Your home, its decorations and atmosphere, are a natural extension of you. Take a good look around your living space. What does it say about you? One of the men I interviewed for this book told of the time he went to pick up a date:

> "While I was waiting for her to get her coat, I looked at her bookcase; it must have had every men-are-assholes paperback ever printed. I forget all the titles, but they were mostly about how stupid it was for women to choose to stay with these terrible men. I mean, there must have been fifteen or twenty of these books; they took up the whole top shelf. They'd obviously been read pretty care-

*fully, too. Made me wonder what kind of an
evening I was in for. It was an okay date, but
nothing ever really came of it; I never called
her after that first date."*

No one's suggesting you shouldn't be able to read
any book you like; just remember that a man who
comes into your home should feel welcome; your living
space should always feel warm and inviting to him. By
the same token, you should try to get an idea of his
personal tastes; be aware of what he orders in res-
taurants or taverns, then try to stock his favorite foods
and drinks at your place. He'll marvel at your intui-
tiveness. (Note also that fresh flowers and candles in
the house are always a plus, as are professionally
laundered linens. You might even splash a little of
your own fragrance around the bedroom; you want to
make a permanent sensory impression.)

STEP THIRTEEN.

Create a history together. Devise nicknames that
have special meaning for just the two of you; plan out-
ings and mystery weekend trips he'll enjoy. Make an
effort to share memorable, pleasant experiences; these
are the stuff of a life shared between two people.

STEP FOURTEEN.

Finally, keep in mind that the best relationships
are going to evolve from a real and sincere friendship.
It will be easier for you to get the commitment if your
date has the opportunity to meet several people who

speak in your behalf and act as your allies. Introduce him to your most pleasant friends (family may be threatening to him). Make sure he meets people in your circle you think he'll get along with; make friends with the people in his life.

CHAPTER EIGHT

Getting Smart with Strategic Planning

*"We must plan . . . or we
must perish."*

— Howard Laski (1893–1950)

What is strategic planning—and how can it possibly fit into your love life?

Strategic planning is knowing where you want to be within a certain time frame and understanding what you have to do to get there. It's putting yourself in the best position in order to accomplish your objectives. Such a concept is more easily applicable to romance than you might think.

You want to be married; you have chosen your man. Now set a time limit for achieving your goal. It may be three months or six months or as long as a year. You will follow a definite strategy in order to achieve your goal. First and most important, you must become acquainted with every person who may become involved in your man's decision making—in short, everyone he may consult before popping the question. Get to know all of these people and, subtly, of course, try to understand their positions with regard to the possibility of his getting married.

THE INSIDE SUPPORT TEAM

An inside support person is anyone who can affect the commitment by wielding influence with your man. In order to achieve your objective, you will need to know the key players, and these could include his mother, his kids, his buddies, his secretary, and, yes, even his ex-wife. These people could prove to be the real decision makers! If your man gets negative feedback about you from all or most of the people he really cares about, he's almost certainly going to step back. So you must pay attention to the people who have an impact on his decisions. Does someone else have to give final, if informal, approval? Does his proposal of marriage need the endorsement and blessing of, say, his children?

If you don't identify the inside support people early on, you could inadvertently offend or bypass someone very influential in your man's life; that's a good way to lose him to someone else. Even when a loving and harmonious match exists between a man and a woman, these inside people can throw a monkey wrench into the proceedings and stop commitment from taking place.

Don't think of inside support people as ogres out to ruin your life; instead, view them as potential helpmates. Remember, you are the "new kid on the block" and they are being asked to make some adjustments to allow you into their world. They, too, love the man you love; they might just be concerned for him, and want to ascertain that you won't hurt him or try to supplant them in his heart. Accordingly, you must try to be as warm, accepting, and nonthreatening to them as you can.

Once you have identified the important people in your man's life, ask yourself the following questions.

- What does each have to offer you as an ally?

- Why might each person perceive you as a potential threat?

- How can you move each person to your side?

You have everything to gain by winning the approval of the inside team. They are part of your man's lifestyle. They will all be affected by his decision. And they will test you.

Children, for example, tend to have a narrow focus. They will wonder what's in it for them. They are not necessarily going to be objective about you, and could easily sabotage the relationship. You will have to walk a fine line.

Money is something else to be aware of. Those close to your man may display selfishness and suspicion if the marriage could affect them financially. (We'll deal with this issue in more depth a little later in this chapter.)

THE MONTHLY REMINDER SYSTEM

Every thirty days, review the status of your relationship just as you would review any personal goal. Ask yourself: What's the potential for commitment?

Let's say that when you selected your eligible bachelor, you set a six-month period for an all-out effort to bring you to a marriage proposal. Two months into the courtship, however, you realize that you're no closer to a proposal than you were when you started. Perhaps you enjoy each other's company, but the emotional closeness you had hoped for has not developed. Or you feel that the relationship is one-sided, with you doing most of the work. He could still be dating other women, or be constantly preoccupied with work, limiting your time together to the weekends and formal dates.

If, for any reason, you believe that the cycle is not progressing as it should, it's time for you to pull back—temporarily. Be friendly, but not so readily available, especially if he's begun to take you for granted. Allow human nature to work on your behalf; men do like to act as the aggressor, and people really do want most what they think they can't have.

It will take a good deal of effort on your part, but be objective in your review. Decide, during this "backing-away" period, whether you will need to come on stronger in the next phase, or perhaps extend the time frame you originally allowed for obtaining your goal. You may have invested too much of yourself too soon, and you may have to change direction somewhat to achieve your objective. Perhaps you should abandon this prospect and find another man more worthy of your time and energy. You may have to go back to your other options.

You need not throw the relationship away entirely, but it's good to remember that a smart single woman never focuses on just one man at a time—until an emotional bond has been established.

FINANCES

Never underestimate the role finances can play in any love match. The financial situation could be the catalyst to bring the man to commit to you . . . or it could destroy the relationship altogether. Be aware of your man's financial commitments.

Money can be a crucial concern, especially if a man is paying alimony and/or child support. He might also be supporting aging parents. For legal reasons, his attorney could advise him against marriage without ever having met you. He may suggest that you sign a prenuptial agreement, especially if you live in a community-property state. (A prenuptial agreement is, of course, completely unnecessary, but ultimately endurable if the man insists on it; it is, however, a prudent cautionary step if the request originates from your side.)

A happily married 42-year-old stockbroker said of his second wife,

> *"Irene was the right person at the right time.*
> *I'm madly in love, but I have three kids in col-*
> *lege. If she weren't financially independent, I*
> *would not have married her."*

Senior citizens have similar concerns. They may lose Social Security benefits if they marry. One man I interviewed faced an interesting situation: his wife had died, and he received $17,000 a year from her estate— until he remarried.

> *"I wasn't about to give that up to marry Mary*
> *Lou if she had no intention of working, just*
> *like I was working,"* he said frankly.

Every man I interviewed said that money was *not* an issue when they were young and getting married for the first time. In second marriages or later-life marriages, however, it is a different story: money becomes a significant factor. The men I interview reported more financial responsibilities, such as child support and tuitions, and thus had more to lose. Of course, financial pressures in marriage are directly responsible for many divorces. Before a possible remarriage, your man's children may worry about their inheritance and his ex-wife may be concerned about retaining her share.

● ● ●

Getting Smart with Strategic Planning

Try to communicate openly and honestly with your man about finances early on so that any complications can be dealt with. You don't want last-minute financial problems to get in the way; you should be aware of each other's expectations and attitudes regarding money.

You already have a frame of reference for his values, having observed his behavior while dating. More than likely he will maintain the same attitude after you are married. For example, if he expected you to split the tab with him on dates, he'll probably want you to share expenses in your married life together. It's best to find out in advance if he expects you to continue to work and share expenses. If you hope to be supported, now is the time to tell him.

Intelligent discussion of financial matters can ward off many later problems. Remember, marriage is a long-term commitment, and your mate's continued satisfaction as well as your own must be a concern.

CHAPTER NINE

Making It Happen

*"It was funny how it all
came together."*

— Chris

You want him to commit. How will you bring the
relationship to its ultimate and gratifying conclusion?

All people successful in relationships are good
listeners. They hear and respond to what their friends
and relatives are really saying. Train yourself to listen
carefully; this is the key. You have already created a
friendly and trusting atmosphere in which your man
feels free to converse with you honestly and confide in
you freely. By listening to his comments and observing
his body language, you will recognize the signals when
he is emotionally ready to commit. Then you will be
ready to lead him toward the proposal.

TIMING

Timing is all-important. In romance you must set a time frame when you are going to expect a proposal or present one yourself. At the first sign of a positive response to your gentle inquiries, you can try to bring your man to make a proposal.

We should be honest here; you don't get that many chances. In any relationship, there will come a critical point at which to go for your objective. How will you recognize it? You must follow your instincts; the signs will be clear enough. When the time is right, when the inside support people are on your side and all objections have been resolved, you must still implement a strategy to get or give a marriage proposal. If you remain sensitive and open to his signals, you will feel when a man's spirit is ready for commitment.

●　●　●

> *"It was funny how it all came together; my folks, who had felt very uneasy and distant with the other girls I'd gone out with, genuinely liked Jeannie; she and I were really in tune with one another. It just felt like the right time to ask her to marry me—and I got the feeling that she knew that, too."* (Chris, a 36-year-old public relations specialist.)

●　●　●

You will be able to tell by his touch, by the way he looks at you, the way he kisses and the way he makes love. At this point in your relationship, you probably know him as well as or better than anyone else. Still, there are some signs to look out for.

SIGNS THAT YOUR MAN IS READY TO COMMIT

ONE.

You are an integral part of his life. He shares his intimate thoughts with you and naturally includes you in his plans. You no longer wonder if you'll be doing something together; it's assumed that you will.

TWO.

He has introduced you to his family and friends. They think of you as a couple, a unit. You are invited together to family functions. You are a secure part of his life.

THREE.

He is a supportive, affectionate friend. He's always there for you, and if either of you has a problem, it is reasonable to assume that you will call upon each other for comfort and solace.

FOUR.

He isn't afraid to show how he feels about you, even

in public. He treats you with respect and introduces you to acquaintances he bumps into unexpectedly when you're out together. He is not vague about your relationship to him when he makes these introductions.

FIVE.

His personal timing is right. Some men simply reach a point in life when they are thinking about getting married, about settling down. You might just be there at the right time. He is ready to share his life.

MOVING IN TOGETHER

I don't recommend your moving in together, because such an arrangement will make it more difficult to get a proposal. If you live with your prospective husband, he will have less reason to make any drastic lifestyle changes. You have already provided him with much of what he wants; what more will he gain by formalizing matters? A trial coupling can turn into a permanent trial coupling that never gets the benefits of a commitment. Important issues like monogamy are often never addressed, although the situation can go on for years and years.

If, however, you do decide to live together without a commitment, set a mutually acceptable time frame to discuss marriage. Don't just continue to live together, thinking he will eventually propose. Tell him you want to be married. Suggest that the two of you review the relationship in three months or six months.

Agree beforehand that at that specified time you'll decide either to split up or to get married. Be sure to set a definite date and adhere to it. You may feel trepidation, fearing that the review will result in a breakup. But if that occurs, it is better to get it over with and continue with your life than wait months—or years—before learning that a marriage proposal is not forthcoming.

THE PROPOSAL

If you do have a campaign to turn a relationship around for yourself, a lot of it will probably depend on finding ways to get the other person to come to the same conclusion on his own. This is not a manipulative situation, but one where positive elements can be highlighted. Until you are certain that there is a commonality between you, you shouldn't tell him your biological clock is running or pressure him about a commitment. This is the place where most women make mistakes.

Instead, once you have established a relationship, accept that it is perfectly valid to say, "What do we have going on here?" or "If a long-term relationship isn't something you're interested in, I don't want to go on."

What I want to do is to show you that once you know *why* men commit, you should be enough in control of your courtship that you can position yourself to ask for a marriage proposal if he doesn't propose to you. How you frame your question depends upon your individual personality and his, but the key to getting married could depend on your taking the initiative.

You must have the conversation in person, for two reasons. First, it's much easier for him to say no over the phone; second, you must have the opportunity to observe his body language and look into his eyes.

If his arms are folded rigidly across his chest and he can't look you in the eyes, you've got trouble. If he acts totally surprised, as though you've been imagining a serious relationship while he was just having fun, this too is a bad sign. But if you've done your monthly reviews and the signs are there for the appropriate timing, he should be receptive to your ideas. In fact, he'll probably even admire you for not being passive.

You might ask, for example, "Where's this relationship going?" Alternatively, you could be a little more forthcoming and simply ask, "Do you think there's a chance we'll ever be married?" If asking questions seems to be inappropriate, you might frame the issue as a statement: "I want to be married" or "Here's my proposal: Let's get married." Your tone and attitude should be quiet, patient, gentle, and loving.

Then exert all your willpower and *stop talking*. Don't tell him what he's thinking. Don't make excuses or apologies for having raised the issue. Don't give advice. Wait; let the words sink in. Too many women in this position get nervous and keep talking. This could unnerve your man and blow your chances. Project confidence; let him fill the silence.

If he makes a positive response (or offers no objections), continue with the discussion. Don't let it drop; seize the moment. Attempt to get the agreement now; you're aiming to take this one out of circulation. Ask him where and when he'd like to get married. Set a date.

CHAPTER TEN

Trial Commitment

"I'm not sure yet."

— Anonymous

At an appropriate moment, when the time is right and the signals are there that your man may be ready to commit, you ask, "How would you like to get married?"—or you might suggest, "I think we should consider getting married." He may reply, "I wouldn't" or "Never again."

In your discussion, how should you handle a negative response? What if you suggest marriage and he says no? Remember that no doesn't necessarily mean never. It could mean, "I'm not sure yet." Or perhaps, "Not now, but maybe in six months."

Ask yourself if it is a qualified no or an absolute no. Your answer will dictate whether you should cut your losses and move on, or patiently give the man more time.

OVERCOMING OBJECTIONS

Do not despair; objections are a good sign. You know exactly what problems or hesitations you're dealing with, and most can be overcome. If he succinctly expresses why he doesn't want to commit, it proves he's been thinking about and considering marriage to you; he just hasn't worked it all out yet.

You have to be ready for the objections and prepared to eliminate all of them. In order to do this successfully, you have to anticipate what he might say. You have to know yourself and be operating from a position of strength and confidence.

If he says he has to think about it, consider this a positive response. It only means he is not totally convinced yet. Don't get angry, don't argue, and don't be aggressive or defensive. Don't register any signs of rejection.

Smile understandingly, be sweet, patient, and persistent. Only then will you prevail. If the discussion dissolves into an argument, if you lapse into tearful frustration, if you make threats, you are setting yourself back. Instead, use this as an opportunity for self-evaluation. Reorganize and try again. Listen carefully to what he is really objecting to. If possible, turn his objections to your advantage. For instance, if he thinks he's too busy with work and personal responsibilities to take on another commitment, offer to lighten his burden and help him out. Instead of feeling trapped, he will feel he has more free time.

If he states a difficult, specific objection—such as a serious dislike of your children—you will need to take a different tack than if he is merely allergic to your cat. There may be unspoken objections that you have to articulate for him. Keep in mind that most relationships are a series of negotiations. No matter how serious or trivial his objections may seem, view them as challenges that can be overcome.

HANDLING PROBLEMS

If he says no, discuss the problem calmly. Is it solvable? For example, if the important people in his life haven't been recruited to your side, you may have a very difficult time changing his mind to act against their objections.

Try to focus on what the real problem is. Make every effort to be objective. Can you and he benefit from outside help, such as going to a marriage counselor? Or is it a case of irreconcilable differences? Is it hopeless?

Weigh the man's merits; is he worth it? You can't force an issue. You have to know when to dismiss him and go on to the next man. But evaluate carefully what happened, and if there was an error on your part, make certain you don't commit the same mistake again.

CONFLICT RESOLUTION

The ability to solve disputes can help a relationship endure. If you and your man cannot come to agreement about issues that create unhappiness when you are together, you may find yourselves going different ways.

Solving conflicts is not a magical gift. It is a learned skill. For this you will each need a pencil and a piece of paper. At a mutually agreed-upon time, sit down at a table and, one at a time, without interruption, air your views. Express your feelings with sentences that begin "I feel" rather than "You do this" or "You should do that." "I feel" sentences are nonthreatening and nonhurtful to the other party.

While your man is speaking his mind, jot down any issues he brings up that you wish to address. When he makes a statement that translates into a problem that needs solving, such as "I feel annoyed when your kids are with you every weekend," jot it down on the paper. When he's finished speaking, it's your turn to speak without interruption, and his turn to write himself notes and jot down issues that need resolution.

Once you have your lists, prioritize them from the most easily solved to the most difficult, knotty problems. Solve the easiest ones first. This will give you a feeling of success, raise your spirits, build a feeling of team spirit, and give you the momentum to tackle the tough conflicts. For example, if it bothers him to take his car every time you go out, and if you don't mind taking your car on excursions, then you can come to an agreement to take turns driving, either on an alternate basis or with another plan that satisfies both of you. If he doesn't like spending time with your children, however, save that for last.

Let him know you are committed to solving the problems and that you'll stay at the table all night, if need be, to get things worked out. If there's an opportunity to inject humor into the discussion, go with it as long as it is not at his expense. Keep the mood light and cooperative.

The thing to keep in mind is that it is easier to solve a bunch of little problems than a big mess that has not been divided into smaller issues. Try to keep the issues as small and manageable as possible, then broach them singly. If one does not resolve itself as easily as anticipated, then skip it, go on to another, and come back to the unsolved problem later.

You are not adversaries here; you are teammates, striving for a common goal of peaceful coexistence. Maintain that attitude, and the disputes should be solved to the satisfaction of both parties.

CHAPTER ELEVEN

In Their Own Words

Men describe commitments that clicked.

> *"When it came, it was
> about five or six
> sentences; that was all."*
>
> — Ryan

A variety of situations from my interviews with men are presented here, with first-person examples of how the successful commitment took place.

Alex—age 30

"We met our first day in college and we dated on and off for four years. Our relationship continued after graduation. We occasionally dated other people, but then things got serious. I knew Sarah wanted to get married—but she never actually said it. I guess I was a little afraid of the whole thing. She moved out of state for six months, then she came back. We lived together for a while, maybe a year. I thought everything had calmed down. Then, out of left field, she told me she had decided to move to Greece. My ego was involved now. I knew she had a thing about Mediterranean men; myself being one and the idea of competition scared me. Before she was scheduled to leave, she finally said she wanted to get married; it was the first time either of us had verbalized it.

"Looking back, I'd have to admit that I'd kind of been taking her for granted. The Greece thing shook me up. She was gone for just two weeks when I sent that fateful telegram asking her to marry me. We've been happily married for three years."

If your man, like Alex, takes you for granted, think of a way to shape him up. Don't be so available, but make it clear that you love him and want to get married. If it's at all possible to create an opportunity for a brief absence, you'll be making use of a very effective tool in determining the direction of your relationship. We all know the "absence makes the heart grow fonder" cliché. A French philosopher once said—and this is a loose translation into English— "Absence is to love as wind is to fire. It extinguishes the small and enhances the great."

Harold—age 44

> "On the third anniversary of us living together, Evelyn asked, 'Are we ever going to get married, or am I always going to be the mistress?' She gave me an ultimatum: she clearly stated that she wanted to be married now; and if my answer was a firm no she intended to end the relationship and move out immediately. Up until then, she had been patient and supportive. My long-running excuse was that I hadn't fully recovered from a bitter divorce.
>
> "I guess you could say Evelyn threw the dice. She put it all on the line; she said she either wanted to know now that we were going to get married or she wanted out of the relationship. I didn't want to lose her. We got married. I think I needed that push."

In this situation, you gamble away everything on the understanding that your relationship is going nowhere and a better person will probably come along if you receive a firm "no." Your man is confronted with proposing marriage or losing you entirely. In this case, Harold wanted to continue to live with Evelyn. He loved her and didn't want to lose her, but he didn't think he wanted marriage. Harold, however, wasn't willing to risk losing Evelyn. He decided to accept her ultimatum; once he came to terms with it, he was more excited and enthusiastic about the idea of getting married than Evelyn was. Harold was able to overcome his fear of marriage—because his terror of losing Evelyn was far greater. They eloped the following weekend.

This can work, but it should be used only when you and your man are on very solid ground. It's the old "bird in the hand" premise. In any gamble, there is always a risk of losing. You have to be fairly certain that your man will go along with your request rather than let you out of his life. In this case, Evelyn wasn't bluffing, and she could have lost everything. Make sure *you're* not bluffing either.

Michael—age 45

"I was sort of ready. I knew what I wanted to do. I think Nora picked up that I was probably ready to settle down. I had a business that was going well, and I was planning to leave it in a year or two when my kids were through college. All I wanted to do was paint; I'm an artist. My life was resolved from that standpoint.

"I'd been involved with several women over the age of 40 who were desperate to be married and had no other direction in their lives. I wanted someone who was bright; I knew Nora was independent, that she wasn't out to get a guy to take care of her. She wasn't looking to get married just for the sake of getting married. We loved each other and the timing felt right so it made sense to me. We were married six months to the day that we met."

This is by far the easiest resolution to a relationship. The man is basically ready to commit, but it's up to the woman to realize that. You won't have to do much to convince him. Be smart; listen. You don't want to ruin your chances by not seizing the moment or by pushing the wrong buttons. He's looking to marry, but he needs help in making up his mind who the woman will be.

Paul—age 34

"Myra made a list of the positives and negatives about our relationship and showed them to me. She said, 'Here's what's good about us and here's what's bad. Let's see which outweighs which.' We had similar goals . . . we were great friends and we had no real problems. She filled certain needs of mine that had not been met before.

"I had to admit that it really was a clear-cut case of the good outweighing the bad. I took a couple of days to think about it, then we set the date that week."

The trouble with this method is that it can work against you. If you are locked in a resolvable conflict, such as geographical proximity, this technique could be helpful. If, however, the problems are more knotty—let's say you want kids, and he is adamant that he doesn't—the situation may worsen by having everything set out in black and white. Of course, one single item can be so outrageous that it destroys the advantages of everything else. But if yours is a clear-cut case of the positives outweighing the negatives, you can win.

Sean—age 42

"Margaret was really the driving force behind it; we'd been seeing each other for a long time; years. I'm embarrassed to say how many. In fact, she was the one who had initiated the relationship. She wanted to get married and start a family. I didn't. She'd set deadlines in the past and when they arrived, nothing happened. She finally said that if we didn't get some counseling about it, she'd consider the relationship finished. So I sprung for this counselor. Cost me $100 a session. At first the only thing I could think about was that I was getting ripped off. I hadn't even said anything. About the third session, though, the shrink said to me, 'Hey, you're a big boy, and you have to decide what you want. Make up your mind. If you want to—marry Margaret. If you don't want to get married, it's time to break off the relationship so you can both go your own way.' I realized that we really were at a crossroads, and that I had to choose. So I chose her and I'm glad I did."

Extreme measures may be required in this type of situation. If your man is too laid back or too lacking in confidence to make a decision on his own, you will have to walk him patiently through the process.

Ryan—age 31

"Paula never really pressured me, not in
the same way you think about women pressuring men to get married. She was just very
clear about what she wanted; not early on in
the relationship, but after about a year or so.
And when it came, it was about five or six
sentences; that was all. She came right out
and said that she wanted to get married. I
really think it would have turned me off if
she'd hemmed and hawed about it, or
dropped little hints; she knows I'm a very
forthright, straight-ahead guy. So she just
said it; she said, 'This relationship isn't going
to work for me if we don't get married.' And I
thought about it for a while and said, 'Yeah, I
can understand how you'd feel that way.'
Then she asked what we ought to do about it,
and I said I needed some time to think, which
I did. We lived on the opposite sides of town;
we were going to spend two weeks apart—
that was her idea—and that really made me
stop and think. I hadn't spent that much time
away from her since we'd starting seeing
each other. So eight or nine days into it, I
called her up and said that I thought it made
sense to me, too. We set a date. And she said,
'Good; now that we've got that out of the way,
why don't you get the hell over here with a
bottle of Merlot. I miss you.'"

As you can see, a gentle prodding should be all you need if your relationship is on solid ground and you are meeting each other's needs.

In all situations, your approach should be friendly, honest and straightforward. If he agrees to commit under severe duress, he may back out later. You want what's best for *both* of you, and you want the commitment to last.

Good luck!

Appendices

Questions You Should Ask A Man Who Hasn't Yet Committed

The following questions do not constitute a checklist; you should not fire them off in rapid succession as a "test" of every potential mate you encounter. You *should* try to work them into the conversation naturally with a man who seems like a serious possibility as a husband, but who has not yet committed. Of course, not all questions will be appropriate to your situation; use your own discretion in determining what questions to ask.

QUESTIONS YOU SHOULD ASK A MAN WHO HASN'T YET COMMITTED

What was lacking in your past relationships?

Remember, one of your objectives is to isolate those elements of past encounters that did not work *from your man's point of view*. Getting the answer to this question will not only help you isolate the kind of man you're dealing with . . . it will also help you identify the items he sees as problem areas.

What is most important to you?

Someone with varied interests, a balanced approach to issues of work, home, and recreation, and a strong sense of self will have no problem answering this for you. Long silences are not a good sign. Neither are responses such as, "My car."

Is there anyone else in your life you're involved with romantically?

No explanation required.

Tell me about your closest male friend.

People who form stable friendships with others of the

same sex are, broadly speaking, better bets to maintain a commitment to a life partner.

What was your favorite teacher in grade school like?

No, you're not fishing for hints about early crushes; you're trying to determine how comfortable your man is talking about his childhood. This is a neutral starting point; the man who "can't remember anything interesting" about the period may have a colorless past . . . or he may have unresolved issues that merit his examination.

(If he is divorced:) What do you think went wrong with your first (or previous) marriage?

"Nothing important," "It was all her fault," or "I don't want to talk about it" all represent danger signs, and pretty serious ones at that. Having had a divorce is no crime, but these are rarely if ever black-and-white affairs, and they certainly fall into the "important" category. Your man should have learned something from the experience. Has he? If not, step back, take a deep breath, and think twice about getting involved with him seriously.

What did you think of the movie Fatal Attraction?

Actress Glenn Close, one of the stars of the film, had

an interesting observation on male responses to this thriller, which concerns a perilous fling her character shares with a married man (played by Michael Douglas). She was quoted as saying that she heard only two basic reactions from all the men who talked to her about the movie: either "It scared the hell out of me" or "That would never really happen." Her opinion was that the latter group of men were far more likely to engage in extramarital affairs. It's an interesting theory; if your man hasn't seen the film, you might find renting the video for an evening together an enlightening experience.

Can we talk about past sexual partners?

Not an easy topic to broach, and certainly not something you should bring up as a conversation-starter on the first date. Nevertheless, this must be asked if things look like they're getting serious. Remember that we are living in a dangerous time when it comes to sexual health. Take appropriate precautions. For more information on discussing these issues, you can call the Sexually Transmitted Disease Hotline at 800/227-8922, or the AIDS Hotline at 800/342-AIDS.

I have a friend who's going out of town for the weekend, and she's asked me to babysit. Want to help?

Again, this is best asked in developed relationships,

and is not recommended if you feel your man may be intimidated by the query. The answer will tell you something about his willingness to share tasks that oh-so-faintly call to mind actual parenthood. If he does decide to spend the weekend with you in this way, you'll have an excellent chance to observe his way of interacting with children—an important factor if you would like to build a family with this person. Even if you do not plan on having children, this activity is an excellent way to get a look at the "real him," and to find out whether or not he really has that sense of humor he's been bragging about. (By the way, you can ask your friend(s) to "require" this favor of you if necessary.)

> *How would you feel about*
> *doing (X) tomorrow night*
> *instead of (Y), as we'd planned?*
> *I just found out that (plausible*
> *reason for doing X instead).*

This is not simply to be capricious; you want to determine your man's ability and willingness to compromise on matters of mutual interest. Of course, that's not the same thing as always getting what you want instead of him getting what he wants; show flexibility in return yourself. You are not really that interested in the outcome of the decision here, but rather with the process by which the two of you manage contrary objectives. *All* successful marriages feature some mechanism to resolve such issues. One warning is in order: Make sure to ask him to change something other than an activity or project that is extremely important to him and has been on his schedule for a long time. You won't gain any meaningful information if you ask him to give up his playoff tickets so you can both go have dinner with your sister-in-law, whom you visited together last week.

I want to be a _____ when I grow up. How about you?

Men who take themselves too seriously will have a tough time with this one. The point is to uncover future aspirations, realistic or otherwise, and—just as important—to find out whether he still has the ability to dream.

Have you ever played a practical joke on someone? Would you? (If "yes":) What kind?

The response here can be quite revealing, for two reasons. First of all, if you are involved with someone who has never played a practical joke and would never even consider doing so, you should know that. Second, you may find that the "jokes" your man has played are benign and in good fun—but you may not. If he shows a tendency toward cruelty or seems to take undue delight in humiliating others, beware. The joke may (and probably will) be on you if you decide to get serious with him.

How would you feel about spending 24 straight hours together without turning on the television even once?

If he says "Forget it," you've got trouble. This activity is an excellent yardstick for those in relationships that are ready to get serious. If you find you can't think of anything to say or do—or, worse, can't stand the sight of each other by the end of the day—imagine what a lifetime with this person would be like.

What do you want out of the next two or three years?

Are there specific goals? An optimistic view of life? A sense of purpose? A confident approach to overcoming current obstacles? Does he mention only work matters? Is he secretive? Are you confident you're getting a good picture of this person's aspirations? Do you share them?

What's the biggest disappointment you ever faced? Why do you think it came about?

Careful—don't allow your inquiries to be seen as a

threat. Present the issue as an instance of intimate sharing: Start off by offering up your answers to these questions, then ask for his. What you are trying to determine is *not* the points at which your man is weak or vulnerable, but his mindset. Viewing "the world at large," "the system," "those idiots at school," or any other similarly amorphous entity as being inherently responsible for one's problems or difficulties is not a good sign. You want to see evidence of personal growth and self-determination. If your man gives an example of having been fired after consistently showing up late for work, but blames everything on other factors that were completely out of his control, you are probably not looking at the most promising candidate for the Positive Thinking Award.

(If he is a father:) How do you feel about your relationship with your kids?

You may or may not get a straight answer, but that's all right; what you're after here is body language. Does he tense up when discussing his kids? Hold his hand over his mouth? Cross his arms? Change the subject? There may be insecurities or problems related to his role as a father that would benefit from discussion.

Do I remind you of anyone in your family?

If your man shows evidence of having significant unresolved anger or other emotional baggage with one or more of his parents, and *if* you remind him a great deal of the parent in question, you could be asking for big trouble by getting married.

What's your best category in Trivial Pursuit?

Revealing indeed! It's not so much that any one category makes or breaks your man as a candidate for marriage, but that he should have some passion about some topic that shows up as at least a perceived expertise in *one* of the categories. If he's never played, sit him down and go head-to-head. There's no truer test of character. (Besides, you want to end up with someone who can handle all those tricky geography questions, don't you?)

Don't you hate having to stay really late at work?

You're trying to get an idea of how often this actually occurs. "Nah, I'm used to it by now" is the response of either a confirmed or a budding workaholic. This may or may not be a negative for you, but you should at least have an idea of what you'll be facing (assuming you don't know already).

Do you want to do a walk-a-thon with me?

Or man the phones at the local public television or

radio fundraiser? Or help out at a rummage sale for a worthy charity? Or volunteer to pitch in on the town cleanup? People with high self-esteem enjoy helping others; hopefully your man will fall into this category. In addition, such pursuits are a great way to build your relationship. (P.S. You both might have a great time.)

What do you think about (a setback or disappointment suffered by a mutual acquaintance)?

You're looking for empathy here. Someone who is indifferent to the misfortunes of others—or, worse, scoffs at such misfortunes as being "what people like that deserve"—may very well have problems showing sensitivity to *you* when you need it.

What would you say if I told you I wanted to start a new business of my own?

Use this only if such a development is a realistic possibility; if it is, do not fail to ask. You will gain insights not only on your man's specific reactions to new business undertakings, but also on important issues relating to finances and personal growth.

Does it bother you that I earn more money than you do?

(Or:)

Does it bother you that I don't earn as much money as you do?

(Or:)

Does it bother you that I don't work?

Important issues that should not be swept under the table. Defuse all such "time bombs" before considering serious commitment.

What do you think about the age difference between us?

Ask this if there is a difference of five years or more. There may be no problem, but then again . . . . Examine any unspoken assumptions or agendas. Are there financial issues that have not been discussed openly? It really will all come out in the wash. Try to be as honest as possible in addressing important issues.

What's your favorite lamb recipe?

These days, you are certainly not presuming too much

if you assume that your future mate may have some culinary prowess. Find out. Anyway, if you are dealing with someone whose idea of a gourmet dinner is chicken franks in day-old hot dog buns with flat ginger ale, you should at least be aware of that.

What do you think are my five most and least attractive qualities?

Make up a parallel list about him, then compare notes. The items on the list will almost certainly not be identical. The resulting discussion will be enlightening—and will provide each of you with some valuable insights on how you see and are seen by the other person.

QUESTIONS *NOT* TO ASK A MAN WHO HAS NOT YET COMMITTED

No, but, I mean, do you really love me? I mean really?

What's your sign?

I sure like diamonds. Big ones. Don't you?

Have I told you about all my former lovers?

What was the lineup in Abbott and Costello's "Who's on First" comedy routine? (Unless you can name them all.)

Come here—do you think I have bad breath? Hhhh.

Ssh—hear that ticking sound? Do you think it's my biological clock?

What is it about you that reminds me of Walter Brennan?

Highlights from the Survey

STATISTICAL SUMMARY

The survey consisted of over 1,000 questionnaires filled out by married men from various geographic regions of the United States. The questionnaires were supplemented by in-person interviews with selected respondents.

AGE

The average age of the respondent was 39.32 years; the average age of the respondent's wife was 37.32 years. In 84 percent of the cases, the husband was of the same age or older than the wife. The greatest age differential among the couples was 25 years, in the case of a man of 59 who had recently married a woman of 84.

PREVIOUS MARITAL STATUS

The previous marital status of the respondents broke down along the following lines.

- For approximately **77** percent of those men responding to the survey, their present spouse was their first married partner.

- For approximately **18** percent of those men responding to the survey, their present spouse was their second married partner.

- For approximately **5** percent of those men responding to the survey, their present spouse was at least their third married partner.

EDUCATION

The educational backgrounds of the respondents broke down along the following lines.

- Approximately **20** percent of those men responding to the survey had a high school education or lower.

- Approximately **53** percent of those men responding to the survey had at least some college education.

- Approximately **27** percent of those men responding to the survey had completed at least some work toward an advanced degree.

LENGTH OF COURTSHIP

The average time husbands reported for the "dating period" previous to a decision by both partners to commit was 2.14 years. The longest reported period was 10 years; there were a number of citations of times less than one week, but these were uncommon.

"WOULD YOU MARRY THE SAME WOMAN AGAIN?"

Each respondent was asked whether he would marry the same woman again; approximately 74 percent responded "yes." Those whose "dating period" was less than one year responded "yes" at a 64 percent rate; those whose dating period was more than one year responded "yes" at a 78 percent rate.

COMPANIONSHIP

Approximately 80 percent of the men responding to the survey listed companionship as of significant importance in deciding to commit.

SEXUAL FULFILLMENT

Approximately 77 percent of the men responding to the survey listed sexual fulfillment as of significant importance in deciding to commit.

LOVE

Approximately 72 percent of the men responding to the

survey identified love as of significant importance in deciding to commit. This factor was the most frequent "write-in" of the entire survey.

OTHER REASONS FOR COMMITMENT

Here are the other major reasons identified as of significant importance in deciding to commit.

- Sense of humor
- Emotional stability
- Appearance
- Intellectual compatibility
- General appearance

SPECIAL NOTE: APPEARANCE

Men responding to the survey were also asked to identify the primary physical characteristics of a woman considered to be attractive. The eyes were identified as the most compelling aspect; over 60 percent of men rated eyes as a woman's most important feature.

SPECIAL NOTE: CHILDREN

Approximately 30 percent of the men responding to the survey felt that children and the desire to have a family was of significant importance in deciding to commit. However, among those men married to a second, third, or later partner, the percent specifying children and the desire to have a family as a significant factor in deciding to commit dropped to 19 percent.

SELECTED RESPONSES FROM THE SURVEY

Following are some of the representative responses to questions posed in the survey. More detailed interview responses can be found in the main section of this book.

"We realized that we accepted each other and wanted to grow and change together."

"My reasons for committing to my second wife were different than those for committing to my first wife. I had more understanding of myself and my needs the second time around."

"What was my reason for committing? She said to. If I didn't, she was going to leave."

"The first time I got married I was far from home and wanted to start a family. The second time, I found someone I knew I wanted to spend my life with."

"We shared a generally relaxed relationship; we enjoyed many things in common and felt supportive of each other."

"My reasons for committing? Timing, love, not wanting to be single . . . and fear that she would leave me if I didn't."

"I wanted something permanent."

"I was given an ultimatum."

"I committed to her because she was challenging, self-motivated, career-oriented, open."

"She was my best friend."

"We had a lot in common; I was finally ready to settle down."

"When we got married, we were very young (mid-20s), and our reasons for staying married were different than now. But now that we're older, even though our values and needs are different, we can still make it work. I would marry her again."

"As for general appearance, bearing—the way it all comes off together—is more important than any of the individual parts."

"She is capable and self-motivated, self-supporting and emotionally secure. I married my best friend!"

"I wanted long-term growth with children . . . As I mature I see the impossibility of the task of finding the 'perfect' mate . . . Total opposites would be a disaster, but small dif-

ferences can and must be worked out for a common, long-term goal. We both want to have a family, yes, but we also want to reach our respective personal goal."

"Physical appearance? I don't think it's that important—but she has all I need."

"We've now been married for 23 years; a lot has changed, but fortunately, we seem to be doing pretty well now. After all that time, I enjoy our sexual relationship even more now than I did when we were first married."

Questionnaire

For those approaching marriage.

How do you feel about your potential marriage partner?

Too often people are insecure about their relationships. They wonder: Is this relationship worth nurturing and preserving, or should I terminate it? I suggest that the following ten questions measure your opinion of the ten critical areas of any relationship and that your answers offer a basis for you to evaluate the current state of your relationship.

A basically secure relationship is not affected by whether or not one has children, whether one has little money or lots of it, or whether one works inside or outside the home. The key to good rapport is where one places one's priorities. I am not speaking of exclusivity here. Priority means that your partner's needs are more important than other people's needs. Buddies, depression, alcohol, television, or other activities can adversely affect a person's priorities and consequently interfere in that person's relationship.

I am suggesting that the following ten areas are crucial aspects of a relationship, more or less in order of importance. Write the answers on separate sheets of paper—but don't share your responses while you are taking the test. Circle the number that in your judgment reflects the current state of the relationship. The lowest number reflects the poorest, while the highest reflects an ideal score. Try to avoid the highest number unless you feel the area deserves an almost perfect rating. Respond to each question separately, then total the score.

Use this exercise as an opportunity to communicate with each other about discrepancies in the responses. Remember, it is as easy to attack and to criticize as it is to distort the score.

This test is worthwhile only if used to open discussions, review current events, renew perspectives on each other, reeducate yourselves on your mate's tendencies, or (last but not least) to reinvigorate your sense of humor.

Ten Key Relationship Questions

1. *Loving, caring, respecting each other.* Available in times of hardship, loneliness, and grief as well as periods of joy. Remembering birthdays and anniversaries. Are you sensitive to each other's needs?

   1. . . . 2. . . . 3. . . . 4. . . . 5. . . . 6. . . . 7. . . . 8. . . . 9. . . .10
   Poor   Needs Some Improvement   Great

2. *A sense of humor:* without it life becomes gray, a real drag. William James suggested that "wisdom is learning what to overlook." Laugh a little. None of us is perfect. (I am certainly not suggesting that you make fun of each other's vulnerabilities.) Do you laugh with each other?

1. . . . 2. . . . 3. . . . 4. . . . 5. . . . 6. . . . 7. . . . 8. . . . 9. . . .10
Poor   Needs Some Improvement   Great

3. *Communication.* People say that if you see a man and a woman together at a resort and they are not talking to each other, they must be married. Or, if they are talking to each other, they may be married, but not to each other. Are you able to have conversations that range from significant to playful? I am not suggesting that even the most mature couples tell all. Sometimes honesty is a way of expressing hostility. When you talk to your partner, does the conversation have a sense of zip and enthusiasm?

1. . . . . . 2. . . . . . 3. . . . . . 4. . . . . . 5. . . . . . .6. . . . . . 7. 8
Poor   Needs Some Improvement   Great

4. *Trust and security.* Are you able to count on the other person?

1. . . . . . 2. . . . . . 3. . . . . . 4. . . . . . 5. . . . . . .6. . . . . . 7. 8
Poor   Needs Some Improvement   Great

5. *Tolerance* for occasional moodiness, depression, craziness, and the ability not to bear a grudge. How capable are you of dealing with the unharmonious aspects of the relationship?

1........2........3........4........5........6
Poor   Needs Some Improvement   Great

6. *Ability to share major interests,* such as religion, politics, recreation, doing mitzvahs. Do you share common interests?

1........2........3........4........5........6
Poor   Needs Some Improvement   Great

7. *Ability to respect differences.* Even when your partner has friends you don't like, you can have some friends separately. Can he (or she) have interests that don't interest you?

1........2........3........4........5........6
Poor   Needs Some Improvement   Great

8. *Excitement in planning for future events.* Vacations, organizing an event, decorating the house, throwing a party. Do you enjoy doing what you do together?

1........2........3........4........5........6
Poor   Needs Some Improvement   Great

9. *Sexual fulfillment.* Is your sex-life mutually satisfying?

    1........2........3.......4........5.......6
    Poor   Needs Some Improvement   Great

10. *Sharing household tasks.* Do you or will you share households chores?

    1.....2.....3.....4.....5.....6.....7.....8....9
    Poor   Needs Some Improvement   Great

How To Use Your Results

A perfect score of 73 points means your partner is an illusion or your perceptions are weak.

A score of between 55 and 63 or more points means that the relationship is in good shape. Here, any category rated poor should be discussed.

A score of between 45 and 55 points probably means that some tensions exist, but they are not necessarily disruptive. This is not a good score if you are not yet married. Work on these discrepancies before you decide to marry.

Under 45: have easy talks. Try to communicate and resolve your differences. If this process brings about an argument, see a counselor. Almost any relationship is salvageable with mutual good intentions.

I have not gathered scientific data to justify my positions, but I can think of no better way of getting couples to talk to each other about critical issues.

APPENDIX D

Bibliography/
Recommended Reading

American Couples: Money, Work, and Sex
   Blumstein, Philip, and Schwartz, Pepper.
   William Morrow, 1983.

The Art of Loving
   Fromm, Erich. Bantam, 1956.

*Between Two Gardens: Reflections on Sexuality
   and Religious Experience*
   Nelson, James B. Pilgrim Press, 1988.

Book for Couples
   Prather, Hugh and Gayle. Doubleday, 1988.

Coping with Single Parenting
   McCoy, Kathleen. NAL, 1987.

The Different Drum
   Peck, M. Scott. Simon & Schuster, 1987.

Do I Have to Give Up Me to Be Loved by You?
   Paul, Jordan, and Paul, Margaret.
   Compcare, 1985.

The Eternal Garden: Secrets of Our Sexuality
   Olds, S.W. Times, 1985.

For Each Other: Sharing Sexual Intimacy
   Barbach, Lonnie. Signet, 1984.

Great Sex
   Penney, Alexandra. G.P. Putnam's Sons,
   1985.

*How to Make Love to the Same Person for the Rest
   of Your Life and Still Love It*
   O'Connor, Dagmar. Doubleday, 1985.

*How to Stubbornly Refuse to Make Yourself
   Miserable about Anything—Yes, Anything*
   Ellis, Albert. Lyle Stuart, 1988.

If You Really Loved Me . . .
   Paul, Jordan, and Paul, Margaret, with
   Hesse, Bonnie. Compcare, 1987.

Intimate Partners: Patterns in Love and Marriage
   Scarf, Maggie. Random House, 1987.

Is There Sex After Marriage?
Botwin, Carol. Little, Brown, 1985.

The Joy of Being Single
Harayda, Janice. Doubleday, 1986.

Like Yourself and Others Will, Too
Twerski, Abraham. Prentice-Hall, 1986.

Living, Loving, and Learning
Buscaglia, Leo. Fawcett, 1983.

The Love Test
Bessell, Harold. Warner, 1984.

Making Love Work
Wanderer, Zev, and Fabian, Erika.
Ballantine, 1978.

Marital Myths
Lazarus, Arnold A. Impact, 1985.

Married People: Staying Together in the Age of Divorce
Klagsbrun, F. Bantam, 1985.

Man's Search for Meaning.
Frankl, Victor. Touchstone, 1984.

Men Who Are Good for You and Men Who Are Bad
Hoffman, Susanna. Ten Speed Press, 1987.

More Joy of Sex
　　Comfort, Alex. Crown, 1987

Necessary Losses
　　Viorst, Judith. Fawcett, 1986.

The New Our Bodies, Our Selves
　　Boston Women's Health Collective. Simon &
　　Schuster, 1984.

On Sex and Human Loving
　　Masters and Johnson, with Kolodny. Little,
　　Brown, 1986.

Raising Your Child to Be Sexually Healthy
　　Leight, Lynn. Avon, 1990.

Rediscovering Love
　　Gaylin, Willard. Penguin, 1987.

*The Right to Feel Bad: Coming to Terms with Nor-
　　mal Depression*
　　Hazelton, L. Dial Press, 1984.

The Road Less Traveled
　　Peck, M. Scott. Simon & Schuster, 1978.

The Second Shift
　　Hochschild, Arlie. Viking, 1989.

Sex for One: The Joy of Selfloving
　　Dodson, Betty. Crown, 1987.

Sexual Awareness: Enhancing Sexual Pleasure
McCarthy, B., and McCarthy, E. Carroll &
Graff, 1984.

Styles of Loving
Lasswell, Marcia, and Lobsenz, Norman.
Ballantine, 1984.

*Swept Away: Why Women Fear Their Own
Sexuality*
Cassell, Carol. Fireside, 1989

Touch Therapy
Colton, Helen. Zebra, 1985.

When Bad Things Happen to Good People
Kushner, Harold S. Avon, 1983.

*Whoever Said Life Was Fair? A Guide to Growing
Through Life's Injustices*
Cohen, Sara Kay. Fireside, 1989.

Why Men Are the Way They Are
Farrell, Warren. Berkley, 1988.

Women Men Love—Women Men Leave
Cowan, Connel, and Kinder, Melvyn. Signet,
1987.

Your Sexual Secrets
Klein, Marty. Berkley Press, 1990.

Index

Index

Age range of survey respondents, 26
Appearance, importance of as male criterion for
    commitment, 27, 34-35, 89, 97
The "Adolescent," 61
Alcohol, 90

"Best friend," importance of as male criterion for
    commitment, 26, 28
Biological "clock," pressures of female, 40, 155
"The Boldly Unavailable," 59
"Buyer's market" theory, inadequacy of, 28

Career goals, 27, 44
Changing the man, wisdom of attempts at, 55, 63
Characteristics sought by men in potential partners,
    17, 26-35, 80-81, 93, 133-142
"The Cheater," 58
Child care, 27

"The Chronic Underachiever," 61
"The Collector," 61
Commitment
— as your primary objective, 17-19
— items that appeared as significant factors in male decision to commit, 28-37
— difference between perceived male criteria and actual male criteria for commitment, 21-37, 27
— items that did not appear as significant factors in male decision to commit, 27
— male patterns for timing decision to commit, 39-46
— strategies for commitment, 36-37, 51-54, 77-83, 85-97, 99- 110, 111-117, 119-125
Committers (profiles of), 67-76
Communication between men and women, 23-25, 40, 89, 117
Companionship, importance of as male criterion for commitment, 26, 28, 45
Complaining, importance of avoiding, 82
Complementary qualities, importance of, 29
Confidence, 87, 94
"The Conqueror," 60
Controlling relationship, importance of, 51, 56

Danger signals, 56-57
Dating services, 78
"Delaying" response, 57
Desperation, importance of avoiding impression of, 80, 92

Differences in male and female senses of humor, 32-33
"The Do-Gooder," 60
"The Dependent," 62
Domestic duties, 27
Driving, 57

"The Egomaniac," 60
Emotional needs, male, 29
Emotional stability, importance of woman's as criterion for male decision to commit, 33
Expectations, unrealistic, 43
External pressures
— as contributors to unwillingness to marry same woman again, 42
— relative unimportance of in decision to marry for second time, 42
Ex-wives, 57
Eyes, importance as factor in female appearance, 35

Family, 57
Fashion, 92
Fidelity, 54
Finances, 28, 45, 115-116
First and second marriages, differing male perspectives, 17, 39- 46
First marriages, 43-44
Fitness, 87
Flattery, importance of recognizing, 48
Flirting, 89

Goal orientation, 96, 103-104
"God," 60
Good lover, male definitions of, 31
"The Great Catch," 59

Happiness of various single/married groups, 81
"The Hider," 59
Homosexuality, 62
Housework, 27
How not to meet eligible men, 78-79
How to Marry a Millionaire, 101
Humor, importance of, 32-33
"Hunter" mentality, 104-105
Huntin, Morton, 81

Ideal weight, 27
Improving self-esteem, 93-97
Independence, 87
Infidelity, 54
Inside support team, 112-114
Interest in other women, male, 56

"The Liar," 58
Lies, 53-55, 58
"Lines" (at various stages of relationship) 47-52
Lilly, Doris, 101
Listening, importance of, 52-56, 103-104
Longevity magazine, 81

Love, importance of as male criterion for
     commitment, 26, 29-30, 45, 86
Love life, taking control of, 23

Makeup, importance of avoiding excessive, 35, 88
Male emotional needs, 29
"The Mama's Boy," 60
Married men, difficulties of involvement with, 53
Men who will commit, 67-76
Men who won't commit, 47-65, 67-76
Misogyny, 62
Moving in together, 122-123
Mysteriousness, 87

Nestbuilding, 108
Narrowing "candidate list," 37, 47-48, 56, 79-80
Needs of men, 39-46, 80-81
Negative patterns in past relationships, 41
Noncommitters, 47-65, 67-76

Objectivity, importance of with regard to managing
     relationships, 25, 48-49
Obstacles to commitment, 18, 40-41, 47-65
Occupations of survey respondents, 26

Parents, 56, 56
Patience, importance of, 40, 42, 47, 105
Perfume, 88

Personal relationships, parallels with professional
    relationships, 18, 82
Personal ads, 78
Possessiveness, 56
Profiles of committers, 67-76
Profiles of noncommitters, 58-65, 67-76
Provocativeness, 87
Physical appearance, woman's
    —as criterion for male commitment, 24-25
PMS (see Premenstrual syndrome)
Pregnancy, 41-42
Premenstrual syndrome, 34
Pressure, when to avoid using, 42
"The Prince of Pain," 58
Professional relationships, parallels with personal
    relationships, 18, 82

Questionnaire for the married and for those
    approaching marriage, 165-170
Questions to ask a man who has not yet committed,
    143-154
Questions not to ask a man who has not yet
    committed, 155-156

Religious backgrounds, 27
Requests that you change your appearance, 56

Scheduling, 57
Seduction, 85-97

Sense of humor, importance of as male criterion in commitment, 32-33

Sensuality, importance of, 31, 86, 88

Second marriages
— male perspectives regarding, 28, 44-46
— motives for marrying the second time, 44

Self-analysis, 95

Setting the wedding date, 119-125, 133

Sex, importance of avoiding being pressured into, 49-52, 75-76, 107

Sex, approaches to by various types of men, 57, 75-76

Sexual fulfillment, importance of, 26, 30-31, 107

Single men, longevity of, 46

Smoking, 92

Socioeconomic backgrounds, 27

Strategies for commitment, 36-37, 51-54, 77-83, 85-97, 99-110, 111-117

Strategies for making yourself lovable, 93-97

"The Substance Abuser," 59

Surprise, importance of, 106

Survey of men's reasons for committing, format, design, and numerical outcomes of, 21-22, 25-26, 157-164

Taking control of one's love life, 23

Therapy, 41

"Time to settle down" mindset, 21, 43, 85

Trial commitments, 127-131

Unrealistic expectations, 43

Unwillingness to marry same woman again, reasons
    behind male, 42

Voice, effectiveness of, 90

Weight problems, 27, 95
Weight-loss programs, 95
When men commit, 39-46
Whining, importance of avoiding, 82
Women men won't commit to, 82-83
"The Woman Hater," 62

About the Author

Susan Curtin Kelley, a former professional model and television writer for such network programs as "Kate and Allie" and "The Thorns," is the author of *Real Women Send Flowers*. Ms. Kelley and her husband live in Sarasota, Florida.